Cataloging Nonbook Materials with AACR2R and MARC

A Guide for the School Library Media Specialist

Second Edition

By Marilyn McCroskey
for the American Association of School Librarians,
a division of the American Library Association

Cover designed by Angela Hanshaw, ALA Production Services. Interior text in Tahoma and Times New Roman.

Printed on 60-pound Finch Opaque, a pH-neutral stock, and bound in 10-pt C1S cover stock by Batson Printing.

The paper used in this publication meets the minimum requirements of American National Standard for Information Sciences—Permanence of Paper for Printed Library Materials, ANSI Z39.48-1992.

ISBN 0-8389-8023-6

Published by:
American Association of School Librarians
a division of the American Library Association
50 E. Huron St.
Chicago, Illnois 60611-2795
To order, call 800-545-2433, press 7

Printed in the United States of America

03   02   01   00   99   5   4   3   2   1

TABLE OF CONTENTS

Acknowledgments   iv

Preface to Second Edition   v

Chapter 1
General Guidelines for Cataloging Nonbook Materials   1

Chapter 2
Common MARC Fields and Subfields for Nonbook Materials   17

Chapter 3
Cataloging Video Formats   41

Chapter 4
Cataloging Filmstrips and Slides   83

Chapter 5
Cataloging Nonprojected Graphics   93

Chapter 6
Cataloging Three-Dimensional Materials   105

Chapter 7
Cataloging Sound Recordings   113

Chapter 8
Cataloging Computer Software   143

Chapter 9
Cataloging Interactive Media   155

Bibliographical References   163

Appendix A
Preview Form for AV Items   165

Appendix B
Variable MARC Fields Often Used for Nonbook Cataloging   167

ACKNOWLEDGMENTS

The author gratefully acknowledges the encouragement and support of Karen Horny, Dean of Library Services at Southwest Missouri State University in Springfield, and Neosha Mackey, Associate Dean of Library Services, in making the second edition of this book a reality. The author also thanks colleagues Karen Letarte and Michelle Turvey, cataloging librarians at Southwest Missouri State University, for their assistance with various Catalog Department duties and for helping to verify information during the author's efforts to finish the second edition for publication before the November 1999 AASL conference in Birmingham. Thanks to Steven Hofmann of AASL for coping with a very large e-mail manuscript file, for patient reformatting, and for quick replies to numerous e-mail questions as deadlines approached. Thanks also to Don Adcock for editing a lengthy and complicated manuscript. Without each of you, this publication would not have been possible.

PREFACE TO SECOND EDITION

Guidelines in this booklet are based on *Anglo-American Cataloguing Rules*, 2nd ed., 1998 revision (commonly called AACR2R), *Library of Congress Rule Interpretations* (LCRI), and on current AV cataloging practice. The author has attempted to summarize and simplify the cataloging process for the various media formats as much as possible without sacrificing important information needed in the school library media center. Now that many school media centers are joining networks and shared databases, it is essential that they follow standard cataloging practice.

As in the first edition of this book, general guidelines for cataloging nonbook items and for creating MARC records are first in the second edition, followed by separate chapters for the various AV formats along with examples for each format. The MARC chapter has been extensively expanded to include more MARC fields, and several examples have been added for each MARC field. The intent is to enable the school library media cataloger to refer to the MARC section in this book for most AV cataloging, rather than having to consult the much more extensive *Bibliographic Formats and Standards* document. However, the cataloger should keep in mind that there are many more possible MARC fields, subfields, and indicators in *Bibliographic Formats and Standards* than in the MARC section of this book. *Bibliographic Formats and Standards* should be consulted as needed, as well as the library system manual.

The second edition has been revised for format integration, which was implemented for MARC cataloging records in 1995. Many more MARC examples have been added to the second edition in an effort to provide more help for the school library media cataloger.

The first edition of this book was based on the assumption that readers may not be familiar with the MARC cataloging format, but would be familiar with catalog cards. Each example in the first edition included both a MARC record and a corresponding catalog card. Now that so many school library media centers have automated catalogs, the second edition is based on the assumption that most readers are probably familiar with the MARC format. One example in each chapter includes a corresponding catalog card to show how the information is transcribed in each format.

Because the fixed field and some MARC fields vary from one library system to another, the MARC examples include only standard fields 0XX through 830. Where there might be some differences from system to system within the MARC fields covered in the second edition, the cataloger is referred to the local system manual.

Examples in the first edition of this book used Library of Congress subject headings. Examples in the second edition use Sears subject headings, except in cases where the only appropriate subject heading is Library of Congress. The second indicator for each 6XX field shows which subject headings are Sears (second indicator 8) and which are LC (second indicator 0). Sears allows "borrowing" of LC subject headings for Sears-based catalogs. Sears subject headings in this book are based on the 16th edition of *Sears List of Subject Headings*, 1997.

The first edition was originally the result of a rather lengthy handout that the author used at an AASL conference workshop session in 1992. After the author received many requests by phone and mail for a copy of the handout, a school library media specialist suggested that the conference handout be expanded into a cataloging manual. The first edition was published only a short time before format integration, which made some of its information obsolete. The author apologizes for the long delay in getting a revision ready for publication. Hopefully the second edition will be more useful since it has much more information than the first edition.

The author began over twenty years ago as a new school library media specialist with no training in nonbook cataloging but more than 2000 AV titles to catalog. An AV cataloging manual would have helped immensely with this cataloging project. The author hopes that this manual will make the cataloging process easier for the busy school library media specialist who cannot buy MARC records for all new AV items and may also need to do retrospective conversion for items already in the collection. The author welcomes users' comments, since nonbook cataloging is continually changing and a 3rd edition of this book will eventually be necessary.

Marilyn McCroskey
Associate Professor of Library Science
Southwest Missouri State University
Springfield, Missouri
October, 1999

CHAPTER 1
GENERAL GUIDELINES FOR CATALOGING NONBOOK MATERIALS

Chapter 1 gives general tips and techniques for cataloging nonbook materials. Guidelines for using **MARC** (**MA**chine **R**eadable **C**ataloging) fields and subfields for nonbook materials are found in Chapter 2. Chapters 3 through 9 are format-specific. References to MARC fields and subfields appear below during discussion of cataloging information needed for nonbook materials. Subfield delimiters appear as the symbol ‡. Refer to Chapter 2 for detailed explanations of the various MARC fields, with examples.

Cataloging Rules

For nonbook materials, follow cataloging rules in *Anglo-American Cataloguing Rules*, 2nd ed., 1998 revision (AACR2R) and *Library of Congress Rule Interpretations* (LCRI). Look in AACR2R for the chapter that covers the specific nonbook format (e.g., Chapter 7 for videos, Chapter 6 for sound recordings, etc.). Also refer to the general cataloging rules in Chapter 1 of AACR2R. Keep in mind that Library of Congress practice occasionally differs from prevailing practice among AV catalogers. When this is the case, it is noted in this book.

Cataloging rules do not cover every possible cataloging situation. AV catalogers make many judgment calls based on their interpretation of AACR2R rules and prevailing AV cataloging practice. Occasionally there is difference of opinion among AV catalogers about how certain rules should be applied.

Book Cataloging vs. Nonbook Cataloging

Cataloging nonbook materials is similar to book cataloging in the general way in which the cataloging record is transcribed. However, cataloging nonbook materials is more complex and time-consuming than most book cataloging. Cataloging records will usually be longer for nonbook materials than for books. Main entry for an AV item is much more likely to be under title than for a book. For nonbook items, a bracketed General Materials Designation (GMD) will follow the Title Proper. Often more subject headings will be used for nonbook materials than for books. Publishers are not usually traced for books, but as a local option, production companies, publishers, and distributors may be traced for nonbook materials. These are a few of the differences between book cataloging and nonbook cataloging.

Ordering and Receiving New AV Materials

When an order is placed for AV items, photocopy the descriptions of the items from the distributor's catalog or flyer and keep these photocopies with the order for later use during cataloging. The photocopied description may be the only available description of the AV item's contents.

When the AV order arrives, make sure the items received were the items ordered. Check for apparent damage in shipping. Examine multi-part items to be sure all components are included. Preview items for cataloging as soon as possible, since some AV companies have a 30-day return policy for replacement of a defective copy or an incorrect title.

Previewing AV Materials

Projected media (videos, filmstrips, slide sets, etc.) should be previewed before they are cataloged to catch technical problems. If sound cassette tapes are not previewed in full, they should be checked to see that the program matches the label, and to be sure that the cassette will play and rewind. Contents of kits should be examined carefully. If there are technical problems with an AV item, or a component is missing, contact the distributor for a replacement.

The cataloger does not need to preview an AV item in its entirety. A student worker or clerical assistant can do this previewing. The previewer can use a form (see page 165) to record the actual running time and to record the digital time (or counter number, with older equipment) for cataloging information in opening and closing credits. Using the previewer's form, the cataloger will need to look at only the beginning and end of projected programs to get bibliographic information needed for the cataloging record. To get information for the Summary Note (MARC field 520), the cataloger should look for a description of the program's contents on the container, in accompanying printed materials, or in the distributor's catalog. If no description is available, the cataloger might need to spot through the program in order to write a Summary Note.

The previewer times the program, using equipment with a digital timer (or a stop watch) to get minutes and seconds. Start timing when the video or audio program begins, and stop timing when it ends. Do not time the leader or tail on a video program or sound cassette. AACR2R rules allow catalogers to accept the running time stated on the item, but this is not always accurate. If possible, time any program that may be used in the classroom.

When more than one program is on a videocassette or videodisc, or there are numbered parts one after the other on the same video, time these segments separately if it is possible that they might be used separately in the classroom. Put the duration of parts in the Contents Note (MARC field 505) after the part-titles.

Many libraries do not time sound recordings, but accept the running time stated on them, since sound recordings can take much previewing time. If there is no running time readily available for a sound recording, the duration can be omitted from the cataloging record. But if the sound recording is likely to be used in the classroom, teachers will appreciate a running time. It is possible to get a close estimate for music sound recordings by totaling individual running times of songs (usually found on label, container, or in accompanying booklet).

How to Catalog Sets

Producers sometimes issue related video programs or filmstrips in sets. There is often a series (set) title for the group of videos or filmstrips, with an individual program title on each. Sometimes the series comes together in a box labeled with the series title. If the programs do not have part-titles, or the part-titles are generic and do not make much sense alone (e.g., **Part 1, Introduction**; **Part 2, Process**; etc.), it is usually best to make one cataloging record for the whole set. Add a Contents Note (505 field) with individual part-titles and running times.

At times a separate cataloging record is needed for each part of a numbered multi-volume AV set with non-distinctive part-titles or no part-titles. When only part of the set is purchased, or it is important for patrons to see a summary for each part, separate cataloging records should be made for parts in a series. The individual programs can be cataloged separately by putting the series title first in the Title Proper area, followed by the part number (MARC field 245 ‡n) and for part-title (245 ‡p) if both are present on the item. Add the GMD (245 ‡h) after 245 ‡p (or after ‡n if there is no ‡p). See examples on pp. 72-75, 80, and 87. If the 245 field contains ‡p, be sure to trace the part-title in MARC field 246.

If each physical part of a set has a distinctive title that can stand alone, the parts should usually be cataloged separately with the series title in the MARC field 440. But if the series title is prominent on the Chief Source of Information, a cataloger may choose to put the series title in MARC field 245 ‡a, followed by the part number (245 ‡n), part-title (245 ‡p), and GMD (245 ‡h). However, especially if the series title is not prominent on the Chief Source, catalogers tend to use the individual program title (part-title) as the Title Proper, with the series title in a 440 field and its part number in 440 ‡v.

Main Entry (MARC fields 1XX)

Most AV items will have a title main entry, because many people have responsibility for the contents. However, if one person is almost single-handedly responsible for creating the item, that person will be the main entry. Here are some examples of nonbook items with main entry under person or corporate body instead of title:

- lecture or presentation by one person on video or sound recording, entered under the speaker
- oral readings (sound recordings) of novels or other literary works, entered under original author with an added entry for the reader
- single musical works (or multiple works) by one composer, entered under composer
- multiple musical works by different composers but performed by one person or group, entered under the performer or performing group
- interviews, entered under the person being interviewed, with an added entry for the interviewer)
- cartographic works, entered under publishing company

A verbatim reading of a novel or play on sound cassette would be entered under its author. But a play on video would <u>not</u> be entered under the original author (traced in MARC field 700 instead) because the work as performed is too far removed from the original written work.

Chief Source of Information and Prescribed Sources

The Chief Source of Information for a specific AV format is the cataloger's <u>first</u> source of cataloging information. Chapters 2-10 of AACR2R define the Chief Source of Information for specific formats in Rule X.0B (Rule 2.0B for books, Rule 7.0B for videos, Rule 6.0B for sound recordings, etc.). The Chief Source of Information for books is the title page, for videocassettes the title frame and credits (or cassette label), for sound recordings the attached label of all parts, for kits all components, etc. For any cataloging record, the Title and Statement of Responsibility must come from the Chief Source of Information or its substitute. Other cataloging information may come from other (prescribed) sources, as specified in Chapters 2-10 of AACR2R.

Until recently, containers were not listed in AACR2R as Prescribed Sources of Information for nonbook items, but were added in the 1998 revision. Sometimes the container is the only source of place and publisher. Most catalogers believed that containers should be legitimate sources of information, and many refused to bracket information from containers. Older MARC records may show brackets in the 260 field for data from a container. These brackets may be removed.

Punctuation

Use the same punctuation rules for AV cataloging as for book cataloging. There is sometimes confusion about whether to end a MARC field with a period when the field ends with a square bracket or parenthesis mark. According to AACR2R and Library of Congress Rule Interpretations, the cataloger ends the MARC 245 field with a period even if the last element is the bracketed GMD. The MARC 250 field also ends with a period even if the edition statement is bracketed. The MARC 260 field does not end with a period if the last element is a bracketed date or a hyphen. The MARC 300 field ends with a period, even if the last element is the physical description of an accompanying guide in parentheses. The 5XX note fields always end with a period even if the period follows a right parenthesis mark.

Title (MARC field 245 ‡a and ‡b)

The Title Proper (245 ‡a) is usually separated from Other Title Information (245 ‡b; usually subtitle) by the General Material Designation (GMD; 245 ‡h). An exception is when the series title is used as Title Proper (245 ‡a, followed by the part number in ‡n and part-title in ‡p, then GMD; see example, p. 87).

Often the title of AV items varies on labels, containers, and accompanying printed material. In the Note Area, use 500 fields to list the variant titles and where they appear. Trace these variations in 246 fields if the difference is in the first five words. If the distributor's catalog lists the item under a title variation, make a 500 note about the variant title and trace it to avoid ordering the item again.

If the title does not come from the Chief Source of Information, add a 500 Source of Title Note. For computer software, this note must always be included, no matter where the title came from. Do not bracket the title in the 245 field unless the cataloger made up the title, as for locally-recorded video or sound recordings with no title on the item and no title available elsewhere.

General Material Designation (GMD) (MARC field 245 ‡h)

The GMD (245 ‡h) follows the Title Proper (245 ‡a) and precedes Other Title Information (245 ‡b, usually subtitle). When the item being cataloged has no collective title but consists of two or three short works (which sometimes happens with music sound recordings), place the GMD after the first title listed (see Rule 1.1C2). This is a recent rule change. Previously, the GMD followed all titles in the 245 field when there was no collective title.

The GMD is always enclosed in its own set of square brackets. Use only the word or phrase specified by AACR2R in Rule 1.1C, List 2. The GMD may or may not be the same term as the Specific Material Designation (SMD) used in the Extent of Item Area of the Physical Description (300 ‡a). See the list on p. 6 for the appropriate terms for GMD and SMD for common media formats.

Note that the list on p. 6 includes the GMD, **[interactive multimedia]**. This GMD does not appear in AACR2R and is expected to change. Also note the spelling disc (previously disk) in the SMD for CD-ROM computer files. This is a recent rule change. Floppies are still spelled disk. For interactive multimedia and other computer files, including World Wide Web resources, a change of GMD is under consideration. If approved, the new GMD for all of these formats will be **[electronic resource]**. Watch for official news on this change, but use **[computer file]** or **[interactive multimedia]** as appropriate until **[electronic resource]** is approved.

The Library of Congress does not use all of the GMDs listed in AACR2R under Rule 1.1C1 (List 2). Other U.S. libraries do use the GMDs on List 2 as a matter of local practice.

GMDs are now used <u>only</u> in the 245 field. Until a few years ago, ‡h [GMD] was used in 740 fields, but ‡h is no longer valid for 740. Older MARC records may use ‡h in 740 fields.

When to Use GMD [kit]

Any group of two or more AV items that comes boxed as a set is not automatically cataloged as a kit. If a set of materials includes more than one medium and <u>one is predominant</u>, catalog the predominant media format and list other components as accompanying materials. For example, a filmstrip with cassette and guide would be cataloged with GMD **[filmstrip]**, not **[kit]**, because the filmstrip is predominant and the cassette and guide are accompanying materials. However, a set including a video, a filmstrip, a record, a puppet, and printed worksheets would be cataloged with GMD **[kit]** because no single medium is predominant.

In a recent rule change, sets of printed materials that must be kept together may also be cataloged with GMD **[kit]**. Examples are testing materials with examiner's manual, student books, and score sheets; and sets of classroom readers with teacher's edition and worksheet masters.

Statement of Responsibility (MARC field 245 ‡c)

This area includes persons with significant overall responsibility, usually <u>writers</u>, <u>producers</u> and <u>directors</u> named in the Chief Source of Information. Transcribe these in the order in which they appear on the item, separated by space-semicolon-space. From the Chief Source of Information, quote exactly the word or phrase which explains that person's role (e.g., **producer, John Smith**; or **produced by John Smith**). If a responsible person's name appears alone on the Chief Source of Information and his role is not clear, a statement of function may be added in brackets in 245 ‡c. Example: **[performed by] Louis Armstrong**. If the name were used alone in 245 ‡c, Louis Armstrong would appear to be the composer, not the performer.

The following responsible persons should appear in the Credits Note (508 field), not in the 245 ‡c: executive producers, directors of photography (or cameramen if there is no director of photography), editors, and composers of background music (in that order). Actors and actresses in dramatic works, and singers in operas, should be put in a 511 Cast Note. Put hosts, narrators, readers, and musical performers in a 511 Performer Note preceding the 508 Credits Note. Occasionally, hosts or narrators are transcribed in the Statement of Responsibility (245 ‡c) if they appear prominently with the title in the opening credits (e.g., [Title] **with Bill Moyers**).

Writers, producers, directors, and responsible persons listed in 511 and 508 notes are usually listed at the beginning and/or end of a projected program. Others listed in the program credits are not put on the cataloging record unless they have major responsibility for the program. Excep-

CORRECT TERMS FOR GMD AND SMD

TYPE OF MATERIAL	GMD (MARC FIELD 245 ‡h)	SMD (MARC FIELD 300 ‡a)
Videorecordings	[videorecording]*	videocassette(s) videodisc(s)
Interactive videos	[interactive multimedia]	videodisc(s) computer disk(s) (for floppy disks
Graphics:		
Filmstrips	[filmstrip]*	filmstrip(s)
Slides	[slide]*	slides
Transparencies	[transparency]*	transparencies
Flash cards	[flash card]	flash cards (or other term such as picture cards, etc.)
Activity cards	[activity card]	activity cards
Pictures	[picture]	(specific terms such as photographs, etc.)
Posters	[picture]	poster(s)
Study prints	[picture]	study print(s)
Flannel board sets	[picture] or [kit] or [game] (depends on item)	(specific terms, or flannel board pieces)
Sound recordings	[sound recording]*	sound cassette(s) sound tape reel(s) sound disc (for record or CD)
Three-dimensional items:		
Realia	[realia]	(name of object)
Models	[model]	model (or descriptive term)
Games	[game]	(list the components)
Jigsaw puzzles	[game]	jigsaw puzzle(s)
Kits	[kit]*	(list the components)
Computer software:		
Floppy disks	[computer file]*	computer disk(s)
Standard compact discs	[computer file]*	computer optical disc(s)
Interactive compact discs	[interactive multimedia]	computer optical disc(s)

Note: The GMDs marked with an asterisk (*) above are currently being used by the Library of Congress. The GMDs not marked with an asterisk are not currently being used by LC. The GMD [computer file] is expected to be replaced by [electronic resource] in the near future. The GMD [interactive multimedia] was never officially approved as a GMD but was allowed as an experimental GMD for use in OCLC records by U.S. libraries. Interactive multimedia formats will be included in the new GMD [electronic resource]. The other GMDs are still approved for use, and are still used by libraries other than LC.

tions: the animator of an animated film and the choreographer of a dance program would appear in the 508 Credits Note. If writers, producers, and directors are found <u>outside</u> the Chief Source of Information, do not put them in 245 ‡c. List them first in the 508 Credits Note.

The Statement of Responsibility (245 ‡c) may also include a company, government agency, or other corporate body with significant responsibility for creating the work. If corporate bodies are transcribed in 245 ‡c, they appear before persons. If the Chief Source of Information gives a statement of function (e.g., **produced by WETA-TV**), use it. If no statement of function is given, the corporate body's name may be used alone in 245 ‡c since its position in the Statement of Responsibility implies responsibility for the contents. Explain the corporate body's responsibility for the program in a 500 note instead of the Statement of Responsibility if its statement of function on the program is more than a few words, or if its statement of function is not from the Chief Source of Information. Do not include corporate bodies on the cataloging record if their only function is funding the production.

Edition (MARC field 250)

Most AV items do not have an Edition Statement (250 field). Often computer files <u>do</u> have an Edition Statement, such as: **Version 1.1**, which is very important. If an Edition Statement appears on an AV item, use it as for books. If not, omit this area.

Publication Area (Imprint) (MARC field 260)

This area usually includes a place (260 ‡a), publisher (260 ‡b), and date (260 ‡c). Occasionally the 260 field may also include a second place and publisher or a place and distributor (added ‡a and ‡b) before ‡c, as follows:

> 260   ‡a **Place of publication** : ‡b **Publisher** ; ‡a **Place of distribution** : ‡b **Distributing company,** ‡c **Date(s).**

If the distributing company's name is given on the item but its function is not stated, add **[distributor]** in brackets after the distributor's name as a statement of function. Example:

> 260   ‡a **San Ramon, Calif.** : ‡b **International Video Network** ; ‡a **Louisville, KY** : ‡b **Ztek Co. [distributor],** ‡c **c1990.**

If the distributor is not stated on the item or in accompanying printed material but the cataloger wishes to include it, add it in brackets with a statement of function. Example:

> 260   ‡a **Van Nuys, Calif.** : ‡b **LIVE Home Video** ; ‡a **[Itasca, Ill.** : ‡b **Distributed by Critics' Choice Video,** ‡c **1993],** c1974.

The date is usually the copyright of the AV item, preceded by the publication date if it is different. The date stated on sound recordings is usually preceded by **p**, not **c**. In projected programs, the copyright often appears in Roman numerals and must be converted to Arabic numerals. When a container for an AV item gives a later copyright than the Chief Source of Information, this is usually the copyright of the package design rather than the copyright of the program. Infer this container copyright as the publication date and put it in brackets without **c**.

Sometimes no date is given on or with the item and a possible date must be supplied, such as **[198-?]**. AACR2R rules do not allow use of the abbreviation **n.d.** for no date. Occasionally the cataloger's only source of date is the release date given in the description of the item in the distributor's catalog. Bracket the date in 260 ‡c if it comes from the distributor's catalog.

Locally recorded programs or programs taped off-air are not <u>published</u> programs and will have no place or publisher, but only the date of recording in 260 ‡c. For programs taped off-air, give the program's copyright date in a 500 note, and include a recording note (518) such as the following: **Copied off-air with permission, Sept. 1992.**

The 260 ‡c for kits and interactive multimedia is the latest copyright found on the item or its components.

Put brackets around any information in the 260 field that is not found on or with the item but supplied from other sources. Follow the general rules for Publication Area found in AACR2R Chapter 1. In this book, see Chapter 3 on video formats and Chapter 7 on sound recordings for more detailed discussion of date and related cataloging problems.

Physical Description Area (MARC field 300)

See the appropriate chapter in AACR2R for the specific format to find examples for the 300 field. In the Extent of Item area (300 ‡a), first give the number of items along with the correct Specific Material Designation (SMD; e.g., 1 sound cassette; 2 videocassettes, etc.; see list on p. 6). For kits, in 300 ‡a list all components since there is no predominant medium, and all components are considered the collective Chief Source of Information.

For AV items with running times, the placement of the running time depends on the format. Give the running time of video programs and sound recordings in parentheses after the SMD. The sound track for filmstrips and slide sets is not part of the primary medium but on an accompanying item, so the running time appears in parentheses after the accompanying sound track in 300 ‡e.

The running time printed on the item, container, or guide, may be accepted, but this could be off by two or three minutes or more. If the running time is not stated on the item but obtained from previewing, round off the minutes/seconds to the next minute <u>up</u>. Exception: if the program is less than five minutes long, record the running time in minutes and seconds. According to a recent interpretation of the rule on running time, if the running time stated on the item is used in the 300 field, transcribe the time <u>as stated</u> rather than rounding to the next minute up. For example, if the duration on the item is stated as **26 minutes, 10 seconds** or **26:10**, transcribe as **(26 min., 10 sec.)**.

In practice, catalogers still tend to round stated minutes and seconds to the next minute up for most formats (especially videos). Cataloging records for sound formats are more likely to show minutes and seconds. Running times for individual songs in 505 are usually recorded as minutes and seconds separated by a colon, such as **(3:27)**. If no running time is stated on an AV item, the Library of Congress does not estimate a running time even though this is an allowed option in AACR2R, Rule 1.5B4c. Most AV catalogers try to provide an actual or estimated running time.

The Other Physical Details area (300 ‡b) varies according to format. For motion pictures and videos, include both sound and color features in 300 ‡b. If there is any sound at all, even just background music, use **sd.** in 300 ‡b. Use **si.** only if there is no audible sound at any time. For projected programs with physically separate sound tracks, such as slides and filmstrips, include only the col./b&w feature in 300 ‡b and put running time in 300 ‡e.

The Dimensions Area (300 ‡c) also varies according to format. For slides and sound cassette tapes, omit ‡c if the item is the standard size. For other formats, some dimensions are stated in inches and others in millimeters. Examples:

    ; ‡c 16 mm. [for motion picture]
    ; ‡c ½ in. [for VHS videocassette]
    ; ‡c ¾ in. [for U-matic videocassette]
    ; ‡c 35 mm. [for filmstrip]
    ; ‡c 4 ¾ in. [for sound or computer CD]
    ; ‡c 3 ½ in. [for small floppy disk]
    ; ‡c 5 ¼ in. [for large floppy disk]

Occasionally catalogers add the dimensions of the container in 300 ‡c. This is often done for kits or for collections of like items (e.g., posters or flannel board pieces) that are of varying sizes. In such cases, instead of putting the dimensions of the cataloged items of the set in 300 ‡c, measure the container in centimeters and transcribe as <u>length x width x depth</u> in 300 ‡c (see example, p. 106).

After Dimensions (300 ‡c), add Accompanying Material in a single ‡e with a plus (+) sign before each accompanying item. Optionally, include physical descriptions of accompanying items in 300 ‡e, such as: **1 guide (48 p. : ill. ; 28 cm.)**, or **1 guide (1 folded sheet)**. In the past, catalogers usually did not add physical descriptions of accompanying items, but now the trend is to add this information. The user can then tell more about the size and extent of the accompanying printed materials.

Series (MARC fields 440 and 490/830)

Many AV items are part of a series (occasionally part of more than one series). Trace the series titles unless a title is a very generic publisher's series. If possible, try to find the Library of Congress form of the series title and follow LC practice. If the series title stated on the item differs from the authorized form, use a 490 field with first indicator 1 for the form of the series title found on the item. Trace the series in its authorized form in an 830 field.

Notes (MARC fields 5XX)

Information for 5XX notes can come from any source, including the guide and the distributor's catalog. If the container does not provide a description and there is no guide, the distributor's catalog description might be the cataloger's only source of information for the Summary Note (520 field).

Look in the appropriate AACR2R chapter for the format as well as AACR2R Chapter 1 for examples of 5XX notes and their order. Nonbook cataloging usually requires several notes. Information in notes does not have to be transcribed exactly as in fields 2XX and 4XX. Following are some types of 5XX notes that are often used for AV items, described in the order in which they should be listed on the MARC record. Not all of these notes will appear on one cataloging record. Occasionally another type of note is needed that is not listed here (see AACR2R). The rules specify the order for notes, but it is permissible to list a note first instead of in the prescribed note sequence if this note is especially important to users. Following are notes often used for AV items, in the order prescribed by AACR2R (see MARC fields in Chapter 2 for examples of each):

- **Format or System Requirements Note (538 field)**

  The format note for videos (e.g., **538 VHS format.**) now should be first in the Note Area. In the past, the video format note was considered a Physical Description Note and appeared just before the 520 Summary Note. The format note is also listed first for sound CDs (**538 Compact disc.**). In cataloging records from vendors and large databases, the Format Note may appear either first or just before the 520. For computer software, the first note is the 538 System Requirements Note.

- **Language Note (546 field)**

  Used to describe the presence of special language features on an AV item, such as foreign language. Also used for video formats to explain the presence of sign language, closed captions, open captions, and audio description.

- **Source of Title Note (500 field)**

  The Source of Title Note tells where the Title Proper was found. For computer software and interactive multimedia, a note for source of title is mandatory. For other formats, the note is used only if the Title Proper is taken from a source other than the Chief Source of Information defined by AACR2R.

- **Variant Title Note (500 field)**

  Notes about title variations (500 field) are needed if the title varies on labels, container, guide, or in the distributor's catalog. These titles are traced in 246 fields.

- **Statement of Responsibility Note: Corporate Body (500 field)**

  If corporate bodies with responsibility for the program do not appear in 245 ‡c, notes explaining their roles will be in 500 fields preceding 511 and 508 notes about people responsible for the program.

- **Statement of Responsibility Note: Cast Note (511 field, 1st indicator 1)**

  A Cast Note is standard for dramatic productions such as plays, feature films, and operas. Library systems automatically supply the word **Cast:** preceding the text of this note on the public screen. Such a word supplied automatically is called a <u>print constant</u>.

- **Statement of Responsibility Note: Performer's Note (511 field, 1st indicator 0)**

  A Performer's Note is standard for music recordings for singers and instrumentalists, and for programs with host, narrator, panelists, or speakers. No print constant is generated with 1st indicator 0.

- **Statement of Responsibility Note: Credits Note (508 field)**

  A Credits Note is standard for projected programs if these persons appear on or with the program. The 508 field may also be used for other formats, such as computer software and sound recordings. Library systems supply the print constant **Credits:** preceding the Credits Note on the public screen. List persons with certain types of technical responsibility, using the following structure:

  > **508 Executive producer(s) ; director(s) of photography or cameramen ; editors ; composers of music.**

- **Edition and History of Publication Note (500 field)**

  Use this note if the AV item was previously issued in another format, or based on a novel or other work.

10

- **Date/Place of Recording (518 field)**

  If information is readily available concerning when and where the program was recorded, use this note.

- **Physical Description Note (500 field)**

  Use 500 fields for notes about physical characteristics and accompanying material that cannot be transcribed in the 300 field.

- **Bibliography or Discography Note (504 field)**

  Use 504 when bibliographical references appear at the end of a video or in its guide, when a discography accompanies a music sound recording, etc.

- **Target Audience Note (521 field)**

  Use the 521 field only when this information is stated on the item, container, or in accompanying material. The 521 field gives intended age or grade level for educational programs, or MPAA rating for motion pictures. Various print constants are possible for the public screen (see Chapter 2 on MARC fields).

- **Summary Note (520 field)**

  A Summary Note (520 field) is needed for AV formats unless there is a Contents Note (505 field) that provides an adequate description, as with collections of music. The 520 Summary Note should be brief and does not have to contain complete sentences, but it should provide essential information and terms useful for keyword search. The blurb on the container or in distributor's catalog can be used as a basis for the 520 Summary Note, but edit out superlatives and sales pitch bias. Library systems supply the print constant **Summary:** on the public screen.

- **Contents Note (505 field)**

  Cataloging records for AV items with separate segments or parts should include a 505 Contents Note giving part-titles (and separate running times if known). Library systems supply the print constant **Contents:** on the public screen.

- **Awards Note (586 field)**

  If an AV item has won awards, and this information is readily available, add a 586 Awards Note. Several different print constants are possible, depending on choice of first indicator.

- **"With" Note (501 field)**

  If the cataloging record is for a program that is physically joined to one or more separately-cataloged programs, list other programs on the physical item in a 501 field. Begin the note **With:** followed by the title of the other program(s) on the item. However, if there is a collective title on the label or container, use the collective title as the Title Proper and list segments in a 505 Contents Note.

Subject Headings (MARC fields 6XX)

AV items usually require more 6XX subject headings than books. AV catalogers often include both specific and more general subject headings, even though the principles of subject cataloging (e.g., Sears) discourage this. AV items are expensive and need the best possible access.

When possible, examples in this book use Sears subject headings (second indicator 8). When Sears does not have an appropriate subject heading and this specific access is needed, a Library of Congress subject heading is shown (second indicator 0). Sears allows such borrowing of LC subject headings as long as there is no conflict with a Sears heading.

Do not assign a subject heading that is just the format (e.g., **Videocassettes**). Do not subdivide a subject heading by format (e.g., **[subject heading]--Videocassettes**). Videos that are closed-captioned, open captioned, in sign language, or audio-described should have an appropriate 650 subject heading for the special feature. For interactive video or multimedia programs, the Library of Congress subject subdivision **--Interactive multimedia** may be added to topical subject headings. Sears does not have a comparable subject subdivision. For more specific information on subject headings for the various formats, see Chapters 3-9 in this book. For specific information on MARC tagging for certain types of subject headings, see the 6XX section in Chapter 2 of this book.

Added Entries (MARC fields 7XX-8XX)

Remember one of the basic principles of cataloging: the basis for any 7XX or 8XX access point should appear somewhere in the descriptive portion of the cataloging record, such as 245 ‡c, 260 ‡b, or a 5XX note.

In 700 fields, trace persons listed in 245 ‡c. Also trace persons listed in 5XX fields who are well-known or have major responsibility for the contents of the item, such as writers, producers, directors, important actors and actresses, speakers, and hosts/narrators seen on-screen. For major motion pictures, also trace composers of music. Use the form of personal name established by the Library of Congress if this is known. If not, follow the rules for headings for persons in AACR2R Chapter 22.

In 710 fields, trace corporate bodies named in 245 ‡c, in 260 ‡b, and in 5XX notes which describe responsibility for the program. Some catalogers trace the distributing company from the 260 ‡b; others do not. When making added entries for corporate bodies, use the form of heading established by the Library of Congress if this is known, or establish headings for corporate bodies using AACR2R Chapter 24.

When creating headings for corporate bodies using AACR2R Chapter 24, usually use the form of the corporate body's name appearing on the Chief Source of Information. Include a term of incorporation (e.g., **Incorporated** or **Inc.**) only if it is an integral part of the name or it is needed to show that it is a corporate body. If there is no term of incorporation or other word (such as **Company**) in the name that indicates it is a corporate body, add a qualifier (explanatory term) in parentheses. Examples are **(Firm)** for companies and **(Musical group)** for musical groups. Write the corporate body's name <u>exactly</u> as stated, including capitalization, punctuation, and abbreviations. AACR2R does not allow abbreviations in 710 fields as in the Publisher's Area (260 field).

Title Access Points

Trace titles of items that have a 1XX main entry by using first indicator 1 in the 245 field. Do not use first indicator 1 if the main entry is under title, or the title will index twice. Trace portions of the 245 title that might be considered a title (such as a catchy subtitle) in 246 fields. Also in 246 fields, trace variant titles listed in 500 fields. If the 245 field includes ‡p, trace that part-title in a 246 field. If the cataloging record includes a 505 Contents Note, part-titles or song titles listed in

505 can be traced using 740 fields with indicators 02. Catalogers may not trace titles listed in Contents Notes if there are too many. Keyword search will locate these titles. Most online catalogs automatically trace titles in ‡c of 700 or 710 fields. If not, add a 740 field for each ‡t in a 700 or 710 field.

Series Title Access Points

If a series title is important enough to be recorded in the Series Area, it should be traced (usually as 440) unless it is merely a generic publisher's series. When in doubt, trace it. If the item being cataloged is an episode from a television or radio series, trace the program series name as a uniform title added entry (730 field) followed by **(Television program)** or **(Radio program)**. Usually do not trace a 730 title additionally in 440. The same title would be traced in 440 (no parenthetical qualifier) if the publisher displays the title on label or container along with a number designation **(program 1, pt. 1, 1,** etc.).

Authority Work for Nonbook Materials

If the cataloger has access to a bibliographic utility that has an authority file based on Library of Congress headings, access points other than Sears subject headings should be checked in the authority file. Subject headings in these large databases are Library of Congress, which may be "borrowed" for a Sears-based system if no Sears subject heading is appropriate. An authority file contains an authority record for each authorized heading. The authority record states the authorized form of a personal name, corporate name, conference name, uniform title, series title, or subject heading in a 1XX field. Some authority records will show cross references: see references in 4XX fields, and/or see also references in 5XX fields. It is harder to find authority records for headings for AV items than for books in authority files of bibliographic utilities, but some will be listed there. If a heading is not in the authority file, check the online catalog portion of the database to see how others have established the heading.

Some school library online catalog systems have an authority file component. This allows the cataloger to create local authority records, and also to download authority records from bibliographic utilities if the library is a member. Authority records in a local system automatically provide see references and see also references for the library's public catalog. These cross references can be of great help to users in finding the correct form of headings for both books and nonbook materials. This book does not address the creation of authority records. Check the library's system manual for detailed instructions.

Copy Cataloging of Nonbook Items

"Copy cataloging" means that the cataloger uses a cataloging record prepared by someone else and edits it to create the local cataloging record. A new AV item sometimes comes with a set of catalog cards that can be used as a basis for the local cataloging record. It may be possible to get MARC records from the distributor or from online databases or CD-ROM databases. Such cataloging records may be helpful, but the cataloger still needs to preview the item and carefully check bibliographic information and access points. Cataloging records from AV companies are not always in AACR2R form. MARC records in large databases may have been created from data sheets without the item in hand, or from eye-readable data without previewing the item. Never accept someone else's cataloging (not even from the Library of Congress) without double-checking all information. Make needed changes and add any subject headings or added entries that local users need.

Additional Resources for Help in Cataloging AV Materials

Detailed instructions for cataloging various AV formats, with many examples showing Chief Sources of Information and corresponding MARC records, are found in:

> Olson, Nancy B. *Cataloging of Audiovisual Materials and Other Special Materials: A Manual Based on AACR2.* Ed. Sheila Intner, Edward Swanson. 4th ed. DeKalb, Ill.: Minnesota Scholarly Press, 1998. 326 p.

It is possible to access the online catalog and the authority file of the Library of Congress via the World Wide Web. LC MARC records can be cut and pasted into the local catalog. The LC authority file will help verify form of heading for personal names, corporate names, and series titles. The URL is: http://lcweb.loc.gov/catalog/. Use the Advanced Search feature for access to the LC authority file.

If it is possible to access OCLC through FirstSearch or other means, more than 40,000,000 MARC records for books and nonbook materials are available. Many OCLC records have Dewey classification numbers. Also of great help is the OCLC authority file, which includes Library of Congress authority records and many additional authority records created by other libraries participating in NACO (National Cooperative Cataloging) projects. Many authority records are added to OCLC by NACO-trained AV catalogers in various libraries. The OCLC authority file also includes Library of Congress subject headings. Most bibliographic records in OCLC use LC subject headings, not Sears headings.

Information such as middle names or birth dates to help break conflicts of identical personal names can sometimes be found through Web access to biographical information in Lexis-Nexis. Corporate bodies often have a Web site that gives the official form of corporate name, and its location. AcqWeb is a Web site that provides access to many library publishing companies' Web pages. The AcqWeb URL is: http://www.library.vanderbilt.edu/law/acqs/acqs.html.

To keep up-to-date on AV cataloging rules and practices, consider joining a national group of audiovisual catalogers, OLAC (Online Audiovisual Catalogers, Inc.). OLAC holds a national conference every other year. The conference offers the participant a choice of four out of many two-hour workshop sessions on cataloging various AV formats, taught by experts. Membership dues are affordable and include a quarterly newsletter with much useful information on new AV rule interpretations and current AV cataloging practices. The newsletter is also available on the Internet, along with other information about OLAC, at the OLAC Web site: http://ublib.buffalo.edu/libraries/units/cts/olac/.

Autocat, an electronic discussion list for catalogers, provides information on various library cataloging rules and practices for books and nonbook materials. Subscribe through: LISTSERV@LISTSERV.ACSU.BUFFALO.EDU. Send LISTERV the command **SUBSCRIBE AUTOCAT <Firstname> <Lastname>**, e.g., **SUBSCRIBE AUTOCAT Janet L Doe**. To confirm the subscription, follow instructions given within 48 hours or the subscription request will be cancelled.

EXAMPLES OF CATALOGING RECORDS FOR NONBOOK MATERIALS

In this book at the end of the chapter for each format (Chapters 3-9) are several examples of MARC records. One MARC example in each chapter also includes a corresponding catalog card. Most AV items require long cataloging records. In card format, cataloging records frequently run to two or three catalog cards. MARC records frequently run to two or three screens, occasionally more.

MARC examples in this book show a space before and after delimiter/letter combinations. Some library systems do *not* space before and after the delimiter/letter signposts. Other library systems require the cataloger to input each subfield on a separate line.

The tagged MARC records created by the cataloger will not appear on the public screen in MARC format. For the public screen, some library systems display the cataloging information like a catalog card. Other systems display the cataloging information with a label for each field, and may rearrange the fields input according to AACR2R order by the cataloger. Most library systems have a "brief" version of the public record with only basic bibliographic information and a "long" public view that shows the entire cataloging record. Usually it is possible locally to designate which fields display on the "brief" view. Notes (5XX fields) may display only on the "long" view. Also, some library systems display 5XX notes in a slightly different order than entered on the MARC record, depending on numeric tags. It may be possible to control the order of notes on some library systems.

NOTES

CHAPTER 2
COMMON MARC FIELDS AND SUBFIELDS
FOR NONBOOK MATERIALS

Cataloging for computerized library catalogs requires knowledge of the **MA**chine **R**eadable **C**ataloging (**MARC**) format. This chapter contains a description of MARC fields frequently used in nonbook cataloging, with examples. Most of these MARC fields are used in book cataloging, but some may be used in a slightly different way for nonbook materials.

Using a coding system of numbers and letters, the MARC format breaks up the data on a cataloging record in a way that a computer can display and access it. Each **field** of information is assigned a number or **tag**. Each field of information is also assigned two **indicators**. These indicators will be either numeric values or blank spaces. Some indicators control access. Be very careful to choose the correct indicators for each field. Some library systems require use of the space bar, not the arrow key, to type "blank" indicators.

Each MARC field of information is divided into **subfields** using a symbol-letter combination as a signpost to tell the computer what is next. The symbol is called a **delimiter** mark. The delimiter mark varies from system to system: e.g., an underline (_); a dollar sign ($); in the OCLC database, a vertical line with two horizontal lines through it (‡). The delimiter-letter signpost does the same job in each system. For example, in all systems the subtitle will be found in the 245 field, subfield b (_b, $b, ‡b etc.). Delimiter-letter signposts do not appear on the public screen. However, if the cataloger inadvertently fails to include the delimiter mark before the letter, the system will print the letter by itself on the public screen. Often a subfield is preceded by a punctuation mark (actually an AACR2R divider mark) such as a space-colon-space, space-semicolon-space, or space-slash-space. The delimiter-letter signpost <u>follows</u> this divider mark.

Online library cataloging systems arrange MARC fields in numerical order from the main entry (1XX) through the series field (4XX) on the MARC cataloging record. The 5XX note fields and 6XX subject heading fields will not appear in numerical order within their own group. AACR2R specifies the order for types of 5XX notes. The cataloger determines the correct AACR2R order for the types of 5XX notes on the cataloging record, and then assigns the appropriate 5XX tag to each one. For an AV item, for example, the sequence of notes could be 538, 500, 511, 508, 500, 520, 505.

Subject headings (6XX fields) are listed on a cataloging record in order of importance. Various types of subject headings have different 6XX tags, so the sequence of subject tags could be any combination, such as 610, 651, 650, 600. In the tracings paragraph of a library catalog card, the 6XX subject fields are numbered with Arabic numerals. The 7XX added entry fields are numbered with Roman numerals in the tracings paragraph of a catalog card. The 7XX fields <u>should</u> be entered in numerical order on the MARC record.

Following are brief descriptions of MARC fields and subfields that are frequently used in cataloging nonbook materials. There are other MARC fields. There are also other indicators and subfields for the MARC fields listed in this chapter. Automated library systems have accompanying manuals that list all of the possible fields, indicators, and subfields for that particular system.

Most MARC fields can be used on cataloging records for books or nonbook materials. Before 1995, certain MARC fields could be used only for certain types of materials. Format integration was implemented in 1995 to make tags and indicators consistent for all formats. Most second indicators for 7XX fields were dropped. Older MARC records (such as those from tapeloads in retrospective conversion projects) may not be updated for format integration. The older format may not affect access, but when the cataloger tries to edit the cataloging record, the system may give error messages. It will then be necessary to update obsolete indicators and subfields.

Following are MARC fields often used for AV formats, with examples. For a comprehensive list of MARC fields and subfields, consult the OCLC Bibliographic Formats and Standards document on the World Wide Web: http://www.oclc.org/oclc/bib/toc.htm.

020   INTERNATIONAL STANDARD BOOK NUMBER (ISBN)

Many AV items (especially videos) now have an ISBN number on label or container. Originally used only for books, the ISBN number is a unique number assigned to an item by its publisher. The ISBN number can eliminate confusion of items with generic titles. Whether to include price (‡c) in the 020 field is a local decision. Often libraries omit price to avoid having patrons question the cost of AV items. One video may cost $19.95 while another may cost $295.00. On the public screen, the 020 field may appear along with 5XX notes, or following place-publisher-date (300 field).

Indicators: Both blank.

Subfields: ‡a ISBN number
                  ‡c Terms of availability (price)

Example:

A feature film on videocassette, Age-old friends, has ISBN number 1-55983-392-0. The video cost $58.74 at the time of purchase. Drop the hyphens and input the ISBN number as follows, with price in ‡c if local policy includes it:

    020   ‡a 1559833920 : ‡c $58.74

028   PUBLISHER NUMBER

This field is used for publisher numbers for sound recordings and videorecordings. Publisher or stock number for other formats should be put in 037. For multiple consecutive numbers, enter first and last number separated by a double-dash. For videorecordings, use first indicator 4 and second indicator 0. For sound recordings, use first indicator 0 and second indicator 2.

Indicators: **1st indicator**
                  0   Issue number
                  4   Videorecording number
                  2nd indicator
                  0   No note, no added entry
                  2   Note, no added entry

Subfields: ‡a Publisher number
                  ‡b Source of the number (usually publisher)

Examples:

   Sound recording:
      028 02   ‡a IGS-004 ‡b Igor Records
      028 02   ‡a 41702T--41704T ‡b Radio Store
      (consecutive numbers are separated by a double dash)
   Videocassette:
      028 40   ‡a FFH 6800 ‡b Films for the Humanities & Sciences

037 SOURCE OF ACQUISITION

Use this field for publisher's number or stock number for AV formats <u>other than</u> sound recordings and videocassettes (those stock numbers are put in 028).

Indicators: Blank.

Subfields: ‡a Stock number
‡b Source of the number (Usually publisher)

Example:
037 ‡a C-SP2 ‡b Wellness Reproductions
(set of cards called S.E.A.L.S. II)

092 LOCALLY ASSIGNED DEWEY CALL NUMBER

Many libraries do not classify AV items but may create location numbers with a format abbreviation followed by an accession number, such as VC138 for the videocassette that is number 138 received. If Dewey call numbers are assigned, use the 092 field.

Indicators: Blank.

Subfields: ‡a Classification number
‡b Rest of call number

Examples:
092 ‡a 973.924 ‡b N654

092 ‡a 953.8 ‡b S85a, Pt. 5

1XX MAIN ENTRY HEADINGS

Most AV items are entered under title due to the multiple responsibility for their creation, but some may have a personal author or corporate author as main entry. If a 1XX field is used, the first indicator for the 245 field should be 1 to trace the title. End the 1XX field with a period unless the last keystroke is a right parenthesis mark or a hyphen.

100 MAIN ENTRY HEADING (PERSONAL NAME)

Personal name as main entry heading for AV is relatively rare, but appropriate in certain circumstances. See Chapter 1, General Guidelines, concerning criteria for choosing a personal name as main entry.

Indicators: 1st indicator
0   Forename (First name only)
1   Single surname (Lastname, Firstname) **(most names)**
2   Multiple (compound) surname (Last Name or Last-Name, Firstname)
2nd indicator
Blank

Subfields: ‡a Name
‡c Title or other word associated with the name
‡q Qualifier (For spelled-out name in parentheses following initials)
‡d Birth-death dates

Examples:
100 0 ‡a Cher, ‡d 1946-

100 1 ‡a Seuss, ‡c Dr.

100 1 ‡a Geisel, Theodor Seuss, ‡d 1904-

100 1 ‡a Wells, H. G. ‡q (Herbert George), ‡d 1866-1946.

100 1 ‡a King, Martin Luther, ‡c Jr., ‡d 1929-1968.

100 2 ‡a Newton-John, Olivia.

110   MAIN ENTRY HEADING (CORPORATE BODY)

Rare for AV, but indicated if the work fits the criteria in AACR2R, Rule 21.1B. More often, a corporate body with responsibility for the contents will be an added entry in a 710 field. For music recordings, a musical group will be the main entry if it performs a collection of works by different composers. For cartographic works, the publishing company will be the main entry.

Indicators: **1ˢᵗ indicator**

1	Jurisdiction name (Political jurisdictions, e.g., states or countries, such as United States)
2	Name in direct order (For all other corporate bodies: e.g., a company, association, musical group, etc.)

2ⁿᵈ indicator

Blank

Subfields: ‡a Name of corporate body
‡b Subdivision of corporate body (Repeatable)

Examples:

110 1   ‡a United States. ‡b Congress. ‡b Senate.

110 1   ‡a Missouri. ‡b Dept. of Conservation.

110 2   ‡a Pennsylvania State University.

110 2   ‡a United States Steel Corporation.

110 2   ‡a Peter, Paul and Mary (Musical group)

110 2   ‡a Rolling Stones.

(Qualifier (Musical group) is not added because AACR2R rules say not to add this qualifier if the group's name is plural)

111   MAIN ENTRY HEADING (MEETING NAME)

Use when a conference or meeting name is the main entry heading. Includes exhibitions, expositions, festivals, athletic contests and scientific expeditions. If a conference name is entered indirectly (under a corporate body), use field 110. If in doubt, enter meeting name in field 111.

Indicators: **1ˢᵗ indicator**

2   Name in direct order

2ⁿᵈ indicator

Blank

Subfields: ‡a Meeting or conference name
‡n Number of meeting or conference
‡d Date of meeting or conference
‡c Location of meeting or conference

Examples:

111 2   ‡a Festival of American Folklife ‡d (1987 : ‡c East Lansing, Mich.)

111 2   ‡a Conference on Language and Communication ‡n (4th : ‡d 1985 : ‡c New York, N.Y.)

111 2   ‡a Olympic Games ‡n (17ᵗʰ : ‡d 1960 : ‡c Rome, Italy)

240   UNIFORM TITLE

Use for uniform titles that follow a personal author main entry (100 field). Identifies an item if it has appeared under varying titles. Brings together records for items entered under personal or corporate names and bearing variant titles. Often used in music cataloging. This uniform title does not end with a period. On a catalog card, it appears between the personal name main entry and the title field and is enclosed in square brackets. Do not enter the brackets on the MARC record.

Indicators: **1st indicator**

       1   Traces uniform title

       2nd indicator

       0   Originally a filing indicator, but initial articles are no longer used, so the 2nd indicator should always be 0.

Subfields: ‡a   Uniform title

       ‡f   Date of publication (if needed)

       ‡k   Form subheading

       ‡l   Language

       ‡m   Medium of performance for music

       ‡n   Number of part or section of a work

       ‡r   Key in which music is written

Examples:

       240 10   ‡a Sonatas, ‡m piano

       240 10   ‡a Symphonies, ‡n no. 9

       240 10   ‡a Trios, piano, strings, ‡n no. 1, op. 49, ‡r D minor

       240 10   ‡a Don Quixote. ‡l English

       240 10   ‡a Adventures of Huckleberry Finn

245   TITLE AND TITLE-RELATED FIELDS

Information in the 245 field must come from the Chief Source of Information or its substitute. Transcription of the Title Proper and Other Title Information (245 ‡a and ‡b) are similar to book cataloging. In addition, AV items always have a General Material Designation (GMD) in ‡h, following ‡a. The GMD is enclosed in its own set of square brackets. For the GMD, use <u>only</u> the word or phrase prescribed by AACR2R, rule 1.1C1 (List 2). Use GMD [kit] for a set of two or more media formats when no single format is predominant (filmstrip with accompanying cassette is not a kit), or for sets of printed materials which must be kept together. The Statement of Responsibility (245 ‡c), lists responsible persons found on the Chief Source of Information. For visual programs such as videos, ‡c lists writers, producers, and directors as they appear in the opening and closing credits. Transcribe their statements of function exactly as found on the item and in the order found. Certain other responsible persons are put in the 508 field. The 245 field ends with a period. The basic structure for the 245 field is:

     ‡a Title proper ‡h [GMD] : ‡b other title information / ‡c statement of responsibility ; statement of responsibility ; [etc.].

Indicators: **1st indicator**

       0   No title added entry (Title is main entry)

       1   Generates a title added entry (Use if 1XX field is present)

       2nd indicator

       0-9   Number of nonfiling characters (how many spaces the computer should ignore in filing). If the first word of the title is not an article, the second indicator is 0. If the first word is **The**, the second indicator is 4 (count the blank space between the article and the next word). Do the same for **A** and **An**, French articles **Le**, **La**, **Les**, etc. Be <u>sure</u> that the second indicator is correct. A title with an incorrect filing indicator will be <u>inaccessible</u> in an online catalog.

Subfields: ‡a Title Proper

       ‡n Volume or part number
       ‡p Part-title
       ‡h GMD (media format in brackets)
       ‡b Other Title Information (Subtitle, parallel title, etc.)
       ‡c Statement of Responsibility

Examples:

245 00   ‡a Long shadows ‡h [videorecording] / ‡c produced, directed, narrated by Ross Spears ; co-writer, Jamie Ross.

110 2   ‡a PC Globe, Inc.

245 10   ‡a MacGlobe ‡h [computer file] : ‡b electronic atlas for the Macintosh computer.

245 00   ‡a Dangerous dieting, the wrong way to lose weight. ‡n Part 3, ‡p Eating disorders ‡h [filmstrip] / ‡c written and produced by Ray Messecar.

245 02   ‡a L'Aigle à deux têtes ‡h [videorecording] = ‡b The two-headed eagle / ‡c un film de Jean Cocteau ; directors, George Danciger and Alexandre Mnouchkine ; script, M.T. Gabon.

100 1   ‡a Brahms, Johannes, ‡d 1833-1897.

245 10   ‡a Two sonatas for clarinet, op. 120 nos. 1 and 2 ‡h [sound recording] ; ‡b Clarinet quintet, op. 115 / ‡c Johannes Brahms.

246   VARYING FORM OF TITLE

This tag was originally used only with serials, but format integration validated 246 for books and AV formats as well. Before format integration was implemented in 1995, all varying titles for books and AV formats were put in the 740 field. Use a 246 field for each variant title added entry. Also add 246 fields with spelled-out versions of numbers, abbreviations, and symbols such as the ampersand (&). The 246 field is also used for portions of titles, such as subtitles in 245 ‡b that might be perceived as the title, and part-titles in 245 ‡p. Do not use 246 for title analytics in the 505 field; use 740 instead. Omit initial articles in the 246 field. Do not end the 246 title with a period. Choice of 246 indicators for nonbook materials is more limited than for book cataloging. Some indicators generate notes specific for books and are thus inappropriate for AV.

Indicators: **1st indicator**

1   Traces the variant title and also generates a Variant Title Note controlled by the second indicator. Use if the automated system supports use of ‡i and places the automatic Variant Title Note in a satisfactory location on the public screen. Some systems may place this note before 538 for the public. Some catalogers do not like this conflict with the correct order for notes and do not use 1st indicator 1 and ‡i. They use 1st indicator 3 and add their own 500 Variant Title Notes.

3   Traces the variant title or portion of 245 title. For variant titles, does not generate a Variant Title Note (this note must be added separately as a 500 field).

2nd indicator

Blank   Use for variant title <u>or</u> for a portion of 245 title stated <u>differently</u> (such as spelled-out numbers, abbreviations, or symbols such as ampersand). In general, second indicator blank is used when no other second indicator is appropriate.

0   Portion of 245 title, such as subtitle (245 ‡b), part-title (245 ‡p), or other phrase within the 245 title that users might think is the title. Use for portion of title quoted <u>exactly</u>. If portion of title to be traced is restated in any way, second indicator should be blank.

Subfields: ‡a   Variant title or portion of 245 title

              ‡b   Other Title Information (usually subtitle). Some online systems will not display the subtitle on the public screen if the ‡b signpost is present. If this is the case,

include the space-colon-space divider but omit the ‡b signpost so that both the title and subtitle display to the public.

‡n   Volume or part number

‡p   Part-title

‡i   Text to appear in Variant Title Note generated for public screen. Use only with first indicator 1. The system will trace the title in ‡a, and in addition the variant title note will be displayed on the public screen. Some AV catalogers use ‡i and some do not, depending on how their system displays the variant title note.

Examples:

246 30 ‡a Eating disorders

(Part-title from: **245 00 ‡a Dangerous dieting, the wrong way to lose weight. ‡n Part 3, ‡p Eating disorders ‡h [filmstrip]**. 1st indicator 3 traces title. 2nd indicator 0 indicates that the 246 field contains a portion of the 245 title quoted exactly)

246 30 ‡a Wrong way to lose weight

(Portion of 245 title for filmstrip in previous example. 1st indicator 3 traces title. 2nd indicator 0 indicates that the 246 field contains a portion of the 245 title quoted exactly.)

246 3 ‡a Five thousand fingers of Dr. T

246 3 ‡a Dr. Seuss's The 5000 fingers of Dr. T

246 3 ‡a Dr. Seuss's The five thousand fingers of Dr. T

246 3 ‡a Doctor Seuss's The 5000 fingers of Dr. T

246 3 ‡a Doctor Seuss's The five thousand fingers of Dr. T

(The 245 title for this video is: **The 5000 fingers of Dr T**. Title on cassette label is: **Dr. Seuss's The 5000 fingers of Dr. T**. 1st indicator 3 traces title. 2nd indicator blank is used for titles for which no other second indicator is appropriate. Blank is the only option here since the 246 titles are not exact quotations of portions of the 245 title. First 246 spells out the number in 245 title. Second 246 is variant title from cassette label. A 500 Variant Title Note must also be added. Third 246 spells out the number in the second 246. Fourth and fifth 246 fields spell out the abbreviation **Dr.**)

246 30 ‡a Flip 'n skip

246 3 ‡a Little Kenny's flip and skip

246 3 ‡a Flip and skip

(The 245 title for this game is Little Kenny's flip 'n skip. 1st indicator 3 traces title. First 246 with second indicator 0 is a direct quote from 245 title. Second 246 spells out the abbreviation for **and**. Third 246 is derived from second 246.)

246 3 ‡a Hong Kong, Macau and Singapore

(The 245 title for this video is Hong Kong, Macau & Singapore. First indicator 3 traces title. Second indicator blank is used since 246 title is not an exact quote from 245 title but merely spells out the ampersand.)

246 3 ‡a Arthritis : ‡b riddle of the joints

(This is a variant title on videocassette label. The 245 title is Riddle of the joints. First indicator 3 traces the variant title. A 500 variant title note must be added as follows: **500 ‡a Title on cassette label: Arthritis : riddle of the joints**.)

246 1 ‡i Title on cassette label: ‡a Arthritis : ‡b riddle of the joints

(Alternate method for previous example if ‡i functions appropriately in the local online system. First indicator 1 traces the title and also generates a note based on ‡i for the public screen. The note will display on the public screen as the 500 Variant Title Note in the previous example, but the note will not end with a period.)

250   EDITION STATEMENT

Use 250 only if an edition statement is found on the AV item; otherwise, omit it. Look for words such as <u>edition</u> or <u>version</u> or <u>revised</u>. For computer software, edition statements are very important, such as **Version 1.2.2,** or **Macintosh version.** Interactive multimedia <u>requires</u> a 500 note telling where the edition statement came from. No other format requires such a note. AV items other than computer formats often do not have an edition statement. The 250 field ends with a period.

Indicators: Both blank.

Subfields: ‡a Edition statement.

Examples:

250	‡a 2nd ed.
250	‡a Rev. ed.
250	‡a Centennial ed.
250	‡a Short version.
250	‡a Version 1.2.2.
250	‡a Macintosh version.
250	‡a Mac/Win version.

256   COMPUTER FILE CHARACTERISTICS

May include the number of data files and logical records and the number of program files and program statements. Some computer software catalogers do not use this field; others do. Some use it only when cataloging Internet resources.

Indicators: Both blank.

Subfields: Only ‡a.

Examples:

256	‡a Computer program (1 file : 200 statements)
256	‡a Computer programs (2 files : 4300, 1250 bytes)
256	‡a Computer data (2 files : 800, 1250 records) and programs (3 files : 7260, 3490, 5076 bytes)

260   PLACE, PUBLISHER, DATE

Most cataloging records for AV items have a single place and publisher; occasionally two places and publishers (repeat ‡a and ‡b). If the distributing company and its place are printed on the item, add the place and distributing company's name in another ‡a and ‡b following publisher, along with its statement of function from the item if one is given. Insert **[distributor]** in brackets after the distributor's name if the function is not clear. Videos and sound CDs frequently have a later copyright date on the container than on the viewed program or CD label. The copyright on the container is usually for the package design. Bracket that date as an inferred publication date and follow it with the copyright of the program (or phonogram date for sound recordings, e.g. **p1991**). Put both publication date and copyright date in a single ‡c (see fourth and fifth examples below). Locally recorded videos and sound recordings are not <u>published</u> items and therefore have no ‡a for place and no ‡b for publisher. Use only ‡c with the date of recording for unpublished videos and sound recordings. The 260 field ends with a period unless the last keystroke is a bracket or hyphen.

Indicators:	Both blank.	
Subfields:	‡a Place (repeatable)	
	‡b Publisher or distributor (repeatable)	
	‡c Date (not repeatable)	

Examples:

260   ‡a Northbrook, Ill. : ‡b Coronet Films, ‡c c1987.

260   ‡a [New York] : ‡b National Film Board of Canada, ‡c [1990?]

260   ‡a [New York] : ‡b National Film Board of Canada, ‡c [199-?]

260   ‡a Princeton, N.J. : ‡b Films for the Humanities & Sciences, ‡c [1994], c1989.

260   ‡a New York, N.Y. : ‡b RCA Victor, ‡c [1991], p1956.
(music sound recording)

260   ‡a Tempe, Ariz. : ‡b PC Globe, Inc. ; ‡a [Lakewood, N.J. : ‡b Distributed by MacWarehouse], ‡c c1991.

260   ‡c 1994.
(for locally recorded video or audio program)

300   PHYSICAL DESCRIPTION

The physical description area varies according to the format. See separate rule chapter in AACR2R for videos, sound recordings, kits, computer software, etc. Interactive multimedia is a relatively new format and is not included in AACR2R (see book, *Guidelines for Bibliographic Description of Interactive Multimedia*). For slides and sound cassettes, omit ‡c if the item is the standard size. Items of accompanying material (e.g., guide, worksheet masters, floppy disk, etc.) are added, preceded by plus (+) signs, in a single ‡e. The 300 field ends with a period.

Indicators:	Both blank.	
Subfields:	‡a Extent of Item	
	‡b Other Physical Details	
	‡c Dimensions	
	‡e Accompanying Material	

Examples:

300   ‡a 1 videocassette (30 min.) : ‡b sd., col. ; ‡c 1/2 in.

300   ‡a 3 videocassettes (88 min.) : ‡b sd., col. with b&w sequences ; ‡c 1/2 in. + ‡e 1 guide (24 p. ; 28 cm.) + 10 blackline masters.

300   ‡1 sound disc (74 min.) : ‡b digital ; ‡c 4 3/4 in.
(for a sound CD)

300   ‡a 2 computer disks : ‡b col. ; ‡c 3 1/2 in. + ‡e 1 user's guide (20 p. ; 16 cm.).

300   ‡a 1 computer optical disc : ‡b sd., col. ; ‡c 4 3/4 in. + ‡e 1 leaflet (8 p. ; 12 cm.).
(for a computer CD or an interactive multimedia CD)

300   ‡a 1 videodisc, 2 computer disks (5 1/4 in.), 1 image directory (92 p. ; 23 cm.), 1 quick reference index (1 folded sheet).
(for interactive multimedia on multiple carriers)

300   ‡a 115 lesson and review cards, 7 dividers, 9 spirit masters, 1 teacher's guide (36 p. ; 20 cm.) ; ‡c in container, 17 x 24 x 9 cm.
(for a kit)

440   SERIES (TRACED)

Most series titles should be traced. Video programs are often part of a series, or occasionally two series. For AV items, the series title may appear on label or container, or in the opening credits of projected programs. Sometimes the series title varies on various parts of the item. If possible, try to find out how the series title has been established by the Library of Congress. If this is not possible, in most cases use the form found on the Chief Source of Information, such the opening credits or cassette label of a video. Use field 440 if the series title on the item appears exactly as the established title of the rest of the items in the series. Use field 490 (first indicator 1) with field 830 to trace the series when the series title found on the item is not the established form of the series title. If a number designation for the series is found on the item, such as **pt. 1** or **vol. 1** or merely **1** without a preceding term, put this information in ‡v. Use the number designation from the item, abbreviated if allowed. Do not add a number designation if none is present. Do not put a period after the series title and do not put parentheses around it. Most online systems supply parentheses if the public screen is formatted like a catalog card.

Indicators: **1st indicator**
Blank
2nd indicator
0   Originally used to indicate non-filing characters, but now initial articles are to be omitted from this field. The second indicator should always be 0.

Subfields: ‡a Series title
‡v Volume number/Sequential designation (e.g., **1, pt. 1,** or **vol. 1**)
‡n Number of part or section
‡p Title of part or section

Examples:
440   0   ‡a English literature on video

440   0   ‡a Video visits. ‡p European collection

440   0   ‡a Videoseminar on nonorganic voice disorders ; ‡v pt. 2

440   0   ‡a Principles of metallography ; ‡v tape 9a

440   0   ‡a Stepping stones, pathways to early development ; ‡v #9

440   0   ‡a Effective behavioral programming ; ‡v 1

440   0   ‡a Mosby's physical examination video series. ‡n Set 2 ; ‡v no. 1

440   0   ‡a Teaching in the quality classroom. ‡n 2, ‡p The three conditions for quality

490   SERIES (NOT TRACED OR TRACED DIFFERENTLY IN 830)

If the series title on the item differs from the form established for items in this series, or if the series is very generic and the cataloger does not want to trace it, a 490 field is used.

Indicators: **1st indicator**
0   Series not traced (Series is displayed on cataloging record but is not an access point. AACR2R now requires that most series titles be traced)
1   Series traced differently (Series title on item is different from established form of series title; series is traced in 8XX field.)
2nd indicator
Blank

Subfields: ‡a Series title
‡v Volume number/Sequential designation

Examples:

490 0 ‡a History videos
(Generic title, not traced)

490 1 ‡a Juex visuals
(Traced as: **830 0 ‡a Visual games.**)

490 1 ‡a Campaigns and elections
(Traced as: **830 0 ‡a Campaigns & elections.**)

490 1 ‡a Developing child
(Traced as: **830 0 ‡a Developing child (Barrington, Ill.)**)

5XX   NOTES

Notes supply information that cannot be given in fields 1XX-4XX of the MARC record. Information for notes can come from any source. The cataloger is not required to use exact wording from the item. Specific tags are assigned to certain types of notes. All other notes are put in a **500** field. The **5XX** tags will not appear in numerical order on the MARC record. The <u>order</u> of the notes should be based on AACR2R, regardless of their numerical tag. See AACR2R Chapter 1, Rule 1.7, and the chapter pertaining to the format being cataloged, such as Chapter 7, Rule 7.7 for videos, Chapter 6, Rule 6.7 for sound recordings, etc., for the order of notes for those formats.

Following is a list of common notes for nonbook materials in the order in which they should appear. A cataloging record will not have all of these notes at once. Other notes may be needed that are not listed here. The various 5XX fields can now be used for all formats. Before format integration, some note fields (e.g., 538) could be used only for specified formats. The order of notes is prescribed by AACR2R, but a note may be moved to first in the sequence if important to the local library. For example, 538 was once considered a Physical Description Note but most catalogers now place it first in the 5XX note sequence. The 5XX fields end with a period.

AACR2R ORDER OF COMMON NOTE FIELDS USED FOR NONBOOK MATERIALS:

538	SYSTEM REQUIREMENTS NOTE
546	LANGUAGE NOTE
500	SOURCE OF TITLE NOTE
500	VARIANT TITLE NOTE(S)
500	CORPORATE BODIES RESPONSIBLE FOR CONTENTS
511	CAST NOTE
511	PERFORMER NOTE
508	CREDITS NOTE
500	EDITION AND HISTORY OF PUBLICATION OR PRODUCTION NOTE
518	DATE/PLACE OF RECORDING
500	HOW ITEM WAS PREVIOUSLY ISSUED
500	PHYSICAL DESCRIPTION NOTE
500	ACCOMPANYING MATERIALS NOTE
504	BIBLIOGRAPHY, ETC. NOTE
521	TARGET AUDIENCE NOTE
520	SUMMARY NOTE
505	CONTENTS NOTE
586	AWARDS NOTE
501	"WITH" NOTE
590	LOCAL NOTE

500 GENERAL NOTES

Used for notes that do not fit into one of the other 5XX fields. For example, a 500 note is used to tell the source of the title in the 245 field. A Source of Title Note is <u>required</u> for computer formats and interactive multimedia, and is used for other materials only if the 245 title did not come from the Chief Source of Information. The 500 field is also used to list variant titles; to describe the responsibilities of corporate bodies; to indicate how an item was formerly issued (as with a video that was first a motion picture or television program); to describe physical characteristics that cannot be recorded in the 300 field; to give added information about accompanying material; etc.

Indicators: Both blank.

Subfields: Only ‡a.

Examples:

500	‡a Title from cassette label.
500	‡a Title on cassette label: Arthritis : riddle of the joints.
500	‡a Produced in cooperation with IWF, Germany.
500	‡a Originally produced for the television series, Nova.
500	‡a Based on: The block book / Elizabeth S. Hirsch, editor.

501 "WITH" NOTE

Use only when cataloging two or more parts separately that are physically part of one video or sound recording with no collective title, such as two unrelated programs on one videocassette, or unrelated spoken recordings on each side of a sound cassette. It is also possible to catalog such items on one bibliographic record as a work without a collective title (this is more often done with music sound recordings). If the two physically joined video programs are unrelated and can stand alone (i.e., each has its own title and beginning/ending credits), it is better to catalog the two programs separately. The same is true of sound cassettes or records with an unrelated program on each side. Begin the note with **With:** followed by the title of the other work on the video or sound recording.

Indicators: Both blank.

Subfields: Only ‡a.

Examples:

501	‡a With: The battle of Gettysburg.
501	‡a With: Symphony no. 5 / Beethoven.
501	‡a With: Peer Gynt (Suite) no. 1-2 / Edvard Grieg -- Till Eulenspiegels lustige Streiche / Richard Strauss.

504 BIBLIOGRAPHY, ETC. NOTE

Note about a bibliography, discography, filmography, and/or other bibliographic references; e.g., at the end of a video program or in accompanying material such as guide. Before format integration, the 504 tag could be used only for book cataloging. When the 504 field is used for AV, cataloging practice places this note after the accompanying materials note. AV catalogers do not place it between the 520 and 505 fields.

Indicators: Both blank.

Subfields: Only ‡a.

Examples:

504	‡a Bibliographical references at end of program.

28

504 ‡a Accompanying guidebook includes content summary of video program and bibliographical references (p. 12).

504 ‡a Booklet inserted in container includes discography (p. 20).

505 CONTENTS NOTE

Use when an AV item contains separate segments or works. For example, use when a video program is divided into two or more separate parts, or when a sound recording contains a number of separate songs or poems. A keyword search will pull up separate titles in this field, as well as composers or authors in individual statements of responsibility (see second example below). Some library systems allow coding (enhancing) the 505 information to access titles and authors listed there. See the system manual for subfields for enhanced 505 notes. Most library systems supply the print constant **Contents:** in the public catalog. If so, do not add this word or it will appear twice. If parts to be listed in 505 begin with a number designation, begin with a lower-case letter such as **vol. 1** or **pt. 1** (see third example below).

Indicators: **1st indicator**
0   Entire contents are listed. (There are additional indicators for incomplete or partial contents, but these are almost never used for AV.)

2nd indicator
Blank   Use unless the system handles enhanced contents notes; see system manual.

Subfields: Only ‡a.
Examples:

505 0   ‡a Solo basic (28 min.) -- Solo whitewater (28 min.) -- Doubles basic (28 min.) -- Doubles whitewater (28 min.).

505 0   ‡a Early in the morning / Paul Stookey (1:33) -- 500 miles / Hedy West (2:46) -- Sorrow / Stookey, Peter Yarrow (2:49) -- This train / Yarrow, Stookey (2:03) -- Bamboo / Van Ronk (2:25) -- It's raining / Stookey, Yarrow (4:20) -- If I had my way / Gary Davis (2:17) -- Cruel war / Yarrow, Stookey (3:26) -- Lemon tree / Will Holt (2:52) -- If I had a hammer / Seeger, Hayes (2:06) -- Autumn to May / Yarrow, Stookey (2:43) -- Where have all the flowers gone / Seeger (3:54).

505 0   ‡a pt. 1 (64 slides, 13 min.) -- pt. 2 (58 slides, 13 min.).

508 CREDITS NOTE

The Credits Note lists persons responsible for certain technical aspects of AV programs. Writers, producers, and directors usually appear in ‡c of the 245 field, but should appear in 508 if found outside the Chief Source of Information. If named on the item or in accompanying material, the following appear in 508 in this order, separated by space-semicolon-space:

Executive producer(s) ; director(s) of photography [or if none is given, list cinematographers] ; editor(s) ; composer(s) of music.

In addition, other persons may be added to the 508 field if their roles are significant to the work, such as the animator of an animated film or choreographer of a dance program. Many names will appear in the opening and closing credits of video programs, but usually the only persons who appear on the cataloging record are those specified for 245, 508, and 511 fields in this book. Those with minor responsibility are not named on the cataloging record, such as assistant directors and assistant producers, sound personnel, etc. Most library systems supply the print constant **Credits:** in the public catalog. If so, don't add it, or it will appear twice.

Indicators: Both blank.

Subfields: Only ‡a.
Example:

    508   ‡a Executive producer, Alan C. Blomquist ; director of photography, Kenneth MacMillan ; editor, Robert L. Sinise ; music, Mark Isham.

511   CAST OR PERFORMER NOTE

Members of the cast and performers of music usually appear in the opening or closing credits of a video, on the container of videos and sound CDs, or in accompanying printed material. List only major members of the cast and major performers. Hosts, narrators, and other major speakers are also listed in a 511 note. A keyword search will bring up these names, but most catalogers trace important persons. Some older MARC records will display obsolete first indicators: 2 (print constant **Presenter:**); or 3 (print constant **Narrator:**). These two indicators are no longer used and those statements of function must be typed. First indicator 1 generates the print constant **Cast:** for the public screen.

Indicators: **1st indicator**

    0   Performer Note (No print constant provided. Note will appear to the public just as typed; includes hosts, narrators, speakers, readers, singers, instrumentalists.)
    1   Cast Note (List actors and actresses in dramatic works, or singers in operas.)

2nd indicator

Blank

Subfields: Only ‡a

Examples:

    511 1   ‡a John Malkovich, Gary Sinise, Casey Siemaszko, Ray Walston, Sherilyn Fenn, Alexis Arquette, Joe Morton, Richard Riehle, John Terry, Noble Willingham.
    (First indicator 1 generates the print constant **Cast:** on public screen)

    511 0   ‡a Narrator, Don Wescott.
    (First indicator 0 does not generate a print constant.)

    511 0   ‡a Canoeists, Bill Mason, Paul Mason ; commentary, Bill Mason.
    (First indicator 0 does not generate a print constant.)

518   DATE/PLACE OF RECORDING

Used for videos and sound recordings if date and/or place of recording is known. Tells when/where the program was recorded or taped off-air.

Indicators: Both blank.

Subfields: Only ‡a.

Examples:

    518   ‡a Recorded in Mar. 1983 at Momaday's home in Tucson, Ariz.

    518   ‡a Taped off-air with permission in Oct. 1993.

    518   ‡a Taped live, Oct. 9, 1997, at the World Trade Club, San Francisco.

520   SUMMARY NOTE

This note is used for all AV items unless the Contents Note (505 field) gives sufficient information about the program. Sound recordings which are collections of songs frequently do not have a Summary Note because the 505 Contents Note gives sufficient information. For other formats, a 520 Summary Note is needed to help users determine whether they can use the AV item. Write summaries with the keyword search feature in mind. Avoid case endings. Information for the summary may be found on the container, in the guide, or in the distributor's catalog. If not, the cataloger may need to spot through the program in order to write the summary. Most systems supply the print constant **Summary:**. If so, do not type this word or it will appear twice on the public screen.

Indicators: Both blank.

Subfields: Only ‡a.

Examples:

520   ‡a Presents a historical perspective on rheumatoid arthritis, emphasizing recent research in Britain and Japan. Shows how arthritis affects the joints. Explains new theories about causes of rheumatoid arthritis. Discusses the malfunction of the immune system as a possible cause. Also discusses the human parvovirus and Lyme disease (carried by ticks) as possible causes of arthritis.

(Summary for a video. Print constant **Summary:** appears on public screen.)

520   ‡a Tells the story of Hatshepsut, the only daughter of Thutmose I's royal wife, who lived in ancient Egypt and eventually became Pharaoh. Discusses her contributions both as a royal leader and as a woman.

(Summary for a slide program. Print constant **Summary:** appears on public screen)

521 TARGET AUDIENCE NOTE

This note is relatively new to AV formats. Previously, information about the intended audience appeared at the end of the 520 Summary Note. The 521 note describes the target audience of the AV item, such as groups of persons or age/grade levels for whom the item is intended. It is also used for the MPAA rating of motion pictures. Catalogers usually use a 521 note only if this information is stated on the item. The first indicator controls the print constant for the public screen. Whether to use print constants is a matter of cataloger preference. Some catalogers avoid print constants. They state all needed information in the 521 note, using first indicator 8. Other catalogers like the print constants for interest and reading levels. If the item states both reading grade and interest age or grade level, choose first indicator based on interest age or grade. Some online catalog systems allow users to limit searches by reading grade level, interest age level, and interest grade level. If this type of search is essential for a library's users, cataloging records <u>must</u> contain a 521 field to be searchable this way.

Indicators: **1st indicator**

Blank   Generates the print constant **Audience:**
0   Interest age level (generates the print constant **Interest age level:**)
1   Interest grade level (generates the print constant **Interest grade level:**)
8   No print constant provided (note will appear exactly as typed)

2nd indicator

Blank

Subfields: Only ‡a.

Examples:

521   ‡a For ages 9-12.
(Prints as: **Audience: For ages 9-12.**)

521   ‡a Adults (age 18 and older).
(Prints as: **Audience: Adults (age 18 and older).**)

521 2   ‡a 7 and up.
(Prints as: **Interest grade level: 7 and up.** Item is of interest to those in 7th grade and up.)

521 2   ‡a K-3.
(Prints as **Interest grade level: K-3.** Of interest to students in kindergarten through 3rd grade.)

521 8   ‡a MPAA rating: R.
(Motion picture rated R. Prints exactly as written, with no print constant.)

538 SYSTEM REQUIREMENTS

Formerly used only for computer software, but authorized for all formats by format integration. The 538 note is required for computer software and interactive multimedia to tell the user what kind of equipment is needed to use the program. For computer software and interactive multimedia, begin the note with **System requirements:**. These words do not begin the 538 field for sound CDs and videocassettes. The 538 note should now be the first 5XX field on the cataloging record. Previously, the 538 note appeared later in the note sequence as a Physical Description Note.

Indicators: Both blank.

Subfields: Only ‡a.

Examples:

    538   ‡a VHS format.
(For a video)

    538   ‡a Compact disc.
(For a sound CD, not a computer CD)

    538   ‡a System requirements: Macintosh PowerBook or any Macintosh with hard drive, 2 MB RAM and large display (640 x 400 or greater); System 6.0.7 or later; HyperCard 2.1 or later.
(For computer formats or interactive multimedia)

546 LANGUAGE NOTE

Use for notes relating to the language of the AV item, including sign language for videos. Also use this field for closed-captioned, open captioned, and audio-described videos. Audio description is a feature found on some videos in which a narrator describes what is seen on the screen for the benefit of visually impaired viewers. The rest of the sound track is unchanged, with the sound effects and dialogue of the original version. Usually audio-described videos are also closed-captioned. Closed-captioned videos do not always have a symbol on the label or container to show that this feature is present. Always keep the VCR's closed-caption feature turned on to identify videos with closed-captioning. For closed-captioned videos, use 650 LC subject heading **Video recordings for the hearing impaired** or 650 Sears subject heading **Closed caption video recordings.** For audio-described videos, the Library of Congress has a 650 subject heading, **Video recordings for the visually handicapped.** Sears does not yet have an equivalent subject heading.

Indicators: Both blank.

Subfields: Only ‡a.

Examples:

    546   ‡a In German.

    546   ‡a In French with English subtitles.

    546   ‡a Closed-captioned.
(This note was previously written as: Closed-captioned for the hearing impaired.)

    546   ‡a Closed-captioned and audio-described.

    546   ‡a Open captioned.

    546   ‡a Signed in American Sign Language.

586 AWARDS NOTE

Information about awards associated with items such as prize-winning documentaries or Academy Award-winning movies. The first indicator controls a print constant.

Indicators: **1st indicator**

Blank   Generates the print constant **Awards:**

8   No print constant

2nd indicator

Blank

Subfields: Only ‡a.

Examples:

586   ‡a Academy Award for Best Picture, 1994.

(Prints on public screen as: **Awards: Academy Award for Best Picture, 1994.**)

586   ‡a Cine Golden Eagle ; Golden Venus.

(Prints on public screen as: **Awards: Cine Golden Eagle ; Golden Venus.**)

586 8   ‡a "Emmy Award for Best Classical Program in the Performing Arts, 1980/81."

(Prints as written, with no print constant)

590   LOCAL NOTE

Field 590 may be used on any cataloging record for information unique to the copy being described. If the information is especially important to local users, place the 590 note first in the order of 5XX notes. In a shared database, it is very important to use field 590, not 500, for notes about an individual library's copy of an item, so that the note will not display on the master record for the database since it may not apply to copies in other libraries.

Indicators: Both blank.

Subfields: Only ‡a.

Examples:

590   ‡a Slide 7 missing.

590   ‡a Inaudible signals on accompanying sound cassette are not synchronized with filmstrip. Use side of cassette with audible signals.

6XX   SUBJECT HEADINGS

To determine appropriate subject headings, ask: "Who needs this and why?" Then select subject headings that will help those users find this item. Do not rely on keyword searching as the primary way to find items by subject. Assign as many subject headings as necessary. End a 6XX subject heading with a period except after a parenthesis mark or hyphen. 6XX subject headings are identified with Arabic numerals in the tracings paragraph of a catalog card.

Second indicator 8 can be used for all types of 6XX subject headings if the local library uses Sears List of Subject Headings as a basis for 650 topical subjects. Examples below use 2nd indicator 8 <u>except</u> for 6XX subject headings from the Library of Congress that do not correspond to a Sears heading.

In general, Sears allows catalogers to "borrow" Library of Congress subject headings if there is no corresponding Sears subject heading. Sometimes Sears subject headings are identical to LC subject headings. But there are some consistent differences, such as dates before names of historical periods in Sears (reverse order in LC) and more inverted subject headings in LC (Sears tries to avoid inverted headings). Sometimes the form of the subject term differs slightly, such as **African Americans** and **Vietnam War** in Sears, and **Afro-Americans** and **Vietnamese Conflict** in LC. Cataloging records obtained from

33

large databases usually use LC subject headings. These LC headings must be checked in the Sears list and changed if needed to avoid conflicts in the local online catalog.

A new MARC subject subdivision has recently been added for 6XX fields: form subdivision ‡v. This subfield is for subject subdivisions for form and genre, such as **Fiction, Drama, Poetry, Maps, Periodicals, Songs and music, Collections, Folklore,** and **Biography**. Use ‡v only if the item being cataloged is this form or genre. Use ‡x if the item being cataloged is about the form or genre. For example, use the 650 subject heading **Indians of North America ‡v Folklore** for a video that is a dramatized Indian myth, but use **Indians of North America ‡x Folklore** for a video about Indian mythology. Current versions of online systems may have to be updated before they will accept or access the new subfield for form subdivision. If the local system will not accept or access ‡v, continue to use ‡x until the next system update.

600 SUBJECT ADDED ENTRY (PERSONAL NAME)

This field is similar to field 100 (personal name as main entry). There are more possible subfields than those listed below. The subfields below are often used with AV items. For personal names, the form would be the same for LC or for Sears. Use 2nd indicator 8 if the Sears List of Subject Headings is used for the local catalog.

Indicators: **1st indicator**
0   Forename (First name only)
1   Single surname (Lastname, Firstname)
2   Multiple surname (Last Name or Last-Name, Firstname)
2nd indicator
0   Library of Congress (LC) subject heading
8   Sears subject heading

Subfields: ‡a Name
‡c Title or other word associated with the name
‡q Qualifier (for spelled-out name in parentheses following initials)
‡d Birth-death dates
‡t Title in author/title subject headings (drop initial articles in all languages)
‡x General subdivision
‡v Form subdivision

Examples:
600 08 ‡a Joan, ‡c of Arc, Saint, ‡d 1412-1431.
600 18 ‡a Wells, H. G. ‡q (Herbert George), ‡d 1866-1946.
600 18 ‡a Lincoln, Abraham, ‡d 1809-1865 ‡v Drama.
600 18 ‡a Steinbeck, John, ‡d 1902-1968 ‡v Film and video adaptations.
600 18 ‡a Steinbeck, John, ‡d 1902-1968. ‡t Of mice and men.
600 28 ‡a Lloyd George, David, ‡d 1863-1945.

610 SUBJECT ADDED ENTRY (CORPORATE NAME)

This field is similar to 110 (corporate name as main entry). There are more possible subfields than those listed below. The subfields below are most often used with AV items.

Indicators: **1st indicator**
1   Jurisdiction name (political jurisdictions, e.g., states or countries, such as United States)

2   Name in direct order (for all other corporate bodies: e.g., a company, association, musical group, etc.)

2nd indicator

0   Library of Congress (LC) subject heading
8   Sears subject heading

Subfields: ‡a Name of corporate body
‡b Subdivision of corporate body (Repeatable)
‡t Title in corporate name/title subject headings (drop initial articles **A**, **An**, and **The** in all languages)
‡x General subdivision
‡v Form subdivision

Examples:
610 18   ‡a United States. ‡b Congress. ‡b Senate.

610 28   ‡a Southwest Missouri State University. ‡b Center for
Social Research.

610 28   ‡a St. Louis Cardinals (Baseball team)

610 20   ‡a Challenger (Spacecraft)
(Library of Congress subject heading for the space shuttle Challenger)

610 28   ‡a Challenger (Space shuttle)
(Note difference between this Sears heading and corresponding LC heading in previous example.)

610 28   ‡a Titanic (Steamship)

610 18   ‡a United States. ‡t Education for All Handicapped Children Act.

611   SUBJECT ADDED ENTRY (CONFERENCE OR MEETING NAME)

This field is similar to 111 (meeting name as main entry). There are more possible subfields than those listed below. The subfields below are often used with AV items.

Indicators: **1st indicator**
1   Name in direct order
2nd indicator
0   Library of Congress (LC) subject heading
8   Sears subject heading

Subfields: ‡a Meeting or conference name
‡n Number of meeting or conference
‡c Location of meeting or conference
‡d Date of meeting or conference
‡x General subdivision
‡v Form subdivision

Example:
611 28   ‡a Olympic Games ‡n (11th : ‡d 1936 : ‡c Berlin, Germany)

630   SUBJECT ADDED ENTRY (UNIFORM TITLE)

Uniform titles bring together cataloging records for the same work when different manifestations (e.g., translations) appear under different titles. Use for an AV item <u>about</u> an anonymous classic, a motion picture, a radio or television program, or other work with a title main entry.

Indicators: **1st indicator**
0   Originally a filing indicator, but initial articles are no longer used for uniform titles, so 1st indicator should always be 0.

2nd indicator

0	Library of Congress (LC) subject heading
8	Sears subject heading

Subfields: ‡a Uniform title
‡l Language
‡n Number designation of a part/section of a work
‡p Name designation of a part/section of a work
‡s Version
‡x General subdivision
‡v Form subdivision

Examples:

630 08   Dead Sea scrolls.

630 08   Beowulf.

630 08   Arabian nights ‡x History.

630 08   Doctor Zhivago (Motion picture)

630 08   I love Lucy (Television program)

630 08   Bible. ‡l English. ‡s Authorized.
(LC subject heading for the King James version of the Bible)

650   SUBJECT ADDED ENTRY (TOPICAL)

Use for subject headings that do not qualify for any other 6XX field.

Indicators: **1st indicator**
Blank
2nd indicator

0	Library of Congress (LC) subject heading
8	Sears subject heading

Subfields: ‡a Subject word or phrase
‡z Subdivision by place
‡y Subdivision by time period
‡x General subdivision
‡v Form subdivision

Examples:

650 0   ‡a Rheumatoid arthritis.
(Library of Congress subject heading. There is no corresponding Sears subject heading.)

650 0   ‡a Vietnamese Conflict, 1961-1975 ‡x Protest movements.
(Library of Congress subject heading for Vietnam War.)

650 8   ‡a Vietnam War, 1961-1975 ‡x Protest movements.
(Note that the Sears subject heading for the Vietnam War differs from the previous LC heading.)

650 0   ‡a Popular music ‡z United States ‡y 1961-1970.
(Library of Congress subject heading. Sears also uses **Popular music** but does not subdivide by date, so 2nd indicator 0 is used.)

650 0   ‡a Cowboys ‡v Songs and music.
(Library of Congress subject heading.)

650 8   ‡a Cowhands ‡v Songs and music.
(Note difference between this Sears subject heading and the previous LC subject heading.)

650 0   ‡a Architecture, Domestic.
(Library of Congress subject heading; LC tends to use inverted headings more than Sears.)

650 8   ‡a Domestic architecture.
(Note difference between this Sears subject heading and the previous LC subject heading.)

651 PLACE AS SUBJECT

Use for geographic subject headings, including political jurisdictions such as countries, states, cities, etc., used as a geographic area, not a government. Also use for natural features such as rivers, lakes, deserts, mountains; national parks; geographic regions such as continents or land masses; celestial bodies such as sun, moon, planets, stars; archaeological sites; parks, cemeteries and other geographic entities not capable of authorship.

Indicators:

1ˢᵗ indicator

Blank

2ⁿᵈ indicator

0   Library of Congress (LC) subject heading

8   Sears subject heading

Subfields:

‡a Subject word or phrase
‡z Subdivision by place
‡y Subdivision by time period
‡x General subdivision
‡v Form subdivision

Examples:

651 0 ‡a United States ‡x History ‡y 1961-1969.
(Library of Congress subject heading.)

651 8 ‡a United States ‡x History ‡y 1961-1974.
(Note that the range of years in Sears differs from the previous LC subject heading.)

651 0 ‡a United States ‡x History ‡y Civil War, 1861-1865.
(Library of Congress subject heading.)

651 8 ‡a United States ‡x History ‡y 1861-1865, Civil War.
(Note that Sears places date range before the name of the historical period, not after, as in the previous LC subject heading.)

651 8 ‡a Springfield (Mo.) ‡x History.

651 8 ‡a Moon ‡x Folklore.

651 8 ‡a Santa Fe Trail.

651 8 ‡a Mississippi River ‡v Fiction.

651 8 ‡a Missouri ‡v Maps.

651 8 ‡a Mount Rushmore National Memorial (S.D.)

651 8 ‡a McKinley, Mount (Alaska)

651 0 ‡a Russia (Federation)
(Library of Congress subject heading.)

651 8 ‡a Russia (Republic)
(Note that Sears uses a different form of geographic name for the Russia resulting from the 1991 breakup of the Soviet Union than in the previous LC subject heading.)

7XX ADDED ENTRY HEADINGS

Fields 700 and 710 are for persons and corporate bodies with responsibility for the contents of an item. The 730 and 740 fields are special types of title added entries (other titles are traced as 246 fields and with first indicator in 245). End a 7XX field with a period except after a parenthesis or hyphen. In the tracings paragraph of a catalog card, 7XX headings are designated with Roman numerals.

700   PERSONAL NAME ADDED ENTRY

This field is similar to the 100 field, personal name as main entry. Make added entries in 700 fields for all persons listed in 245 ‡c that are not main entries. Also make 700 added entries for composers of music for major motion pictures, hosts and narrators seen on-screen, interviewers, and readers of talking books. Unseen narrators are usually not traced unless they are otherwise well known as actors/actresses or as important experts in their fields. In addition, consider tracing important actors/actresses, performers, musicians, etc. found in 511 fields. Use judgment concerning which of these persons are important enough to trace. Keyword search will locate them if they are not traced. Most systems access ‡t of the 700 field on routine title searches. Check the system manual to be certain this is true. If not, then a title in 700 ‡t will need to be traced in a 740 field also. But if a 740 field is added and the system <u>does</u> access ‡t on a title search, the title will be accessed twice.

Indicators: **1st indicator**
0 Forename (First name only)
1 Single surname (Lastname, Firstname) **(most names)**
2 Multiple (compound) surname (Last Name or Last-Name, Firstname)
2nd indicator
Blank Use if 700 field is <u>not</u> an author/title analytic (a part of the work being cataloged). Blank will be used most of the time.
2 Use only if 700 field <u>is</u> an analytic (contains ‡t)

Subfields: ‡a Name
‡c Title or other word associated with the name
‡q Qualifier (for spelled-out name in parentheses following initials)
‡d Birth-Death dates
‡t Title in author/title added entries (drop initial articles **A, An,** and **The** in all languages)

Examples:
700 1 ‡a Mason, Bill, ‡d 1929-
700 2 ‡a Park-Fuller, Linda Marguerite.
700 1 ‡a Tolkien, J. R. R. ‡q (John Roland Reuel), ‡d 1892-1973.
700 12 ‡a Seuss, ‡c Dr. ‡t There's a wocket in my pocket.
(Contained in the item being cataloged)

710   CORPORATE BODY ADDED ENTRY

This field is similar to the 110 field, corporate name as main entry. Trace corporate bodies with responsibility for the contents of the work in 710 fields. These corporate bodies may appear in 245 ‡c, or in a note. For AV, also trace corporate bodies listed in the 260 field. Some catalogers do not trace distributors that are not stated on the item but are bracketed in the 260 field; others do.

Indicators: **1st indicator**
1 Jurisdiction name (political jurisdictions, e.g., states or countries, such as United States)
2 Name in direct order (for all other corporate bodies: e.g., a company, association, musical group, etc.)
2nd indicator
Blank
Subfields: ‡a Name of corporate body
‡b Subdivision of corporate body (Repeatable)
‡t Title in corporate name/title added entries (rare)

Examples:

710 2 ‡a Films for the Humanities (Firm)

710 2 ‡a WGBH (Television station : Boston, Mass.)

710 2 ‡a British Broadcasting Corporation. ‡b Television Service.

710 1 ‡a United States. ‡b Congress. ‡b House.

711 CONFERENCE OR MEETING NAME ADDED ENTRY

This field is similar to field 111, conference name as main entry. Use when a conference or meeting name is an added entry heading.

Indicators: **1st indicator**

2   Name in direct order

2nd indicator

Blank

Subfields: ‡a Meeting or conference name

‡n Number of meeting or conference

‡c Location of meeting or conference

‡d Date of meeting or conference

Examples:

111 2 ‡a Festival of American Folklife ‡d (1987 : ‡c East Lansing, Mich.)

111 2 ‡a Conference on Language and Communication ‡n (4th : ‡d 1985 : ‡c New York, N.Y.)

730 UNIFORM TITLE ADDED ENTRY (e.g., TV program)

Use for uniform titles as added entries. These may include journals and newspapers; motion pictures, and radio and television programs (e.g. a video that was previously a television program, or a sound recording that was previously a radio program).

Indicators: **1st indicator**

0   Formerly a filing indicator, but initial article is no longer used in 730 and first indicator should always be 0.

2nd indicator

Blank   Not an analytic

2   Analytical entry (part of work being cataloged)

Subfields: Only ‡a.

Examples:

730 0 ‡a Nova (Television program)

730 0 ‡a Fibber McGee & Molly (Radio program)

740 TITLE ADDED ENTRY (ANALYTIC OR RELATED)

Before format integration was implemented in 1995, this field was used for all variant title added entries. For AV materials, the title often varies on the title frame, label, container and guide. Format integration has defined the 246 field for variant titles, limiting the 740 field to title analytics (such as titles in the 505; use second indicator 2) and related titles (such as title of the work on which the item in hand was based; use second indicator blank). Older MARC records may show ‡h with a GMD following the 740 title, but ‡h is no longer valid for any field except 245 and should be deleted.

Indicators: **1st indicator**

0   Formerly a filing indicator, but initial article is no longer used in 740 and first indicator should always be 0.

39

2nd indicator

Blank   Title is not an analytic (e.g., it is a related title)

2   Analytical entry (part of work being cataloged, e.g. listed in 505 Contents Note)

Subfields: ‡a Title

‡n Volume or Part Number

‡p Part-Title

Examples:

740 02   ‡a Doubles whitewater.

(One of four separately titled segments on a video with a collective title.)

740 0   ‡a Block book.

(Book on which the filmstrip in the 245 field was based.)

830   SERIES ADDED ENTRY (UNIFORM TITLE)

Used if the series tracing differs from the series statement (field 490) or is in a 5XX note. Unlike the series title in the 440 field, the series title in the 830 field ends with a period (except following a right parenthesis mark).

Indicators: **1st indicator**

Blank

2nd indicator

0   Formerly a filing indicator, but initial article is no longer used in 740 and first indicator should always be 0.

Subfields: ‡a Uniform title (series as traced)

‡n Number of part or section

‡p Title of part or section

‡v Volume number/Sequential designation

Examples:

830 0   ‡a Developing child (Barrington, Ill.)

830 0   ‡a Ascent of man. ‡l Spanish ; ‡v no. 5.

CHAPTER 3
CATALOGING VIDEO FORMATS

Refer to Chapter 1, "General Guidelines for Cataloging Nonbook Materials," for general guidelines that apply to video formats. Following is some additional information that is format-specific.

AACR2R Rules for Video Formats

Use the cataloging rules in AACR2R Chapter 7, and refer also to the general rules in AACR2R Chapter 1. Chapter 7 covers videocassettes, videodiscs, and motion pictures.

Previewing

Video formats should be previewed if possible so that a defective copy can be replaced, and also to get an accurate running time. Previewing a video program in its entirety catches technical problems, such as tracking problems that defy adjustment, problems with sound track, blank-outs on video portion, incomplete program (cuts off before end), and faulty or missing closed-captioning. Tracking problems can be due to incompatibility with a particular VCR, so try the video in another VCR before requesting a replacement video.

Previewing may not be possible with videodiscs. A videodisc player may not be available in the library. If not, use the eye-readable data on the videodisc for cataloging information, but be aware that the title frame on the program might not be the same. Programs on videodisc are often available also on videocassette, with the same title and date problems. Preview videodiscs if at all possible. When the cataloger uses a videodisc player to locate credits, it may be more difficult to scan for cataloging information on a videodisc than on a videocassette. The videodisc player might not have a pause feature or it might not show the picture while on pause. It may be difficult to fast-forward search and thus the cataloger might not be able to see the end credits easily. At least check the title frame and opening credits. Check all credits if possible.

A cataloging assistant can preview video formats. It helps the cataloger if the previewer uses a previewing form (see page 165) to record running time and location of credits needed for cataloging. If possible, use a television/video player combination with a built-in digital timer that displays the time on-screen. A remote control with a pause feature is <u>essential</u>. Always hit the rewind button after inserting the videocassette to be sure the video is completely rewound. When sound is heard or images appear on the screen, <u>reset</u> the digital timer. Do not time the blank screen before or after the program. Do time the copyright statement at beginning or end, since producers intend for viewers to see it.

Before beginning a previewing session, always check the video player to be sure that the closed-captioning feature is turned on. The closed-captioning feature may go off if power is interrupted. Closed-captioned videos usually have a **CC** symbol (or a symbol like a TV screen with a tail) on screen or label, but sometimes there is no indication on label or container that the video is closed-captioned, and this is discovered during previewing.

Originally created for hearing-impaired viewers, closed captions display the text of the spoken sound track. Closed captions appear <u>only</u> if the VCR's closed caption feature is turned on. They usually appear near the bottom of the screen as light-colored or white letters on a black strip.

Watch for missing or faulty closed-captioning (incomplete, part garbage, or not in synch with speaker). If the closed-captioning is faulty, or missing when it should be present, contact the distributor for a replacement. Unfortunately, sometimes the video master is defective also. On the cataloging record, be sure to indicate closed-captioning in a 546 field, and also add a 650 subject heading for this feature. It should be possible for hearing-impaired viewers to pull up a list of such videos from the online catalog.

Some closed-captioned videos are also audio-described. Audio description is a relatively new type of video enhancement for visually impaired viewers. An additional narrator describes what is seen on-screen, working around and between the original sound track. For example, the audio description's narrator may say, "A young blonde girl in a blue-and-white gingham dress smiles as she pats a small brown dog," but the original dialogue and other sound at that point is unchanged. Audio description cannot be turned off and may seem distracting to those not accustomed to it. A library may wish to purchase both versions of a videocassette, one with audio descriptions and one without. If a video is closed-captioned and audio described, add appropriate 650 subject headings for these features.

Like closed captions, open captions also display the text of the spoken sound track (not on a strip). Open captions cannot be turned off. Open captions usually appear at the bottom of the screen in a similar manner to English subtitles on a movie with foreign dialogue. If uncertain whether the video is closed-captioned or it has open captions or subtitles, fast-forward search with the picture visible. Open captions and subtitles will remain visible. Closed captions will either disappear altogether or flash by intermittently as garbage on fast-forward search. Open captions and subtitles should be indicated in a 546 note. Open captioned videos should have an appropriate subject heading, such as the LC subject heading **Video recordings for the hearing impaired**. Sears has a subject heading for closed-captioned videos, but does not yet have an appropriate subject heading for open captioned videos.

Look at all of the opening credits, title frame, etc. The title frame is usually in the first minute of the program, but it may not appear until a few minutes into the program, especially for feature films. Use the remote to freeze information needed for cataloging. Most VCRs will freeze-frame for only a short time before turning the video off, so information must be recorded quickly. Preview at the computer so that cataloging information can be typed on the MARC record as it appears on the TV screen.

Always look at the end of the videocassette program. Often most of the responsible persons and the copyright date are in the end credits—except for feature films, where important responsible persons may be scattered throughout the first five or six minutes. Some educational video programs (especially those produced by corporations and professional organizations) may have <u>no</u> responsible persons in opening or closing credits. Other educational videos may list only two or three of the responsible persons that are usually included on a cataloging record: writers, producers, directors, executive producers, directors of photography, cameramen, editors, and composers of music. Occasionally some of these responsible persons are found only in accompanying material or on the container.

When both sound and picture disappear, note the digital time and round to the next minute up for the duration in 300 ‡a. If there is no printed description with the program, it may be necessary to spot through it in order to get information for the 520 Summary Note. The spoken introduction to an educational video program often gives a brief synopsis of what the program will cover.

Chief Source and Prescribed Sources of Information

For video formats, the Chief Source of Information is the program itself: the opening credits, which usually include the title frame; and the end credits, which may list writers, producers, and directors (if these are not at the beginning), as well as persons to be listed in the Credits Note (508 field) and Cast or Performer's Note (511 field).

If there is no title frame, or if the title on the title frame is incorrect or incomplete, or if the item is a videodisc that cannot be previewed, use the information printed on the label attached to the item and consider the label as the substitute Chief Source of Information. If the needed cataloging information is neither on the program nor on the cassette or disc label, use one of the following sources as substitute Chief Source of Information (in this order): accompanying textual material (such as a guide); container for the videocassette (plastic or cardboard); or other sources such as the distributor's catalog.

If the 245 source of title is other than the title frame, make a 500 note telling where the title came from. If there is no title on the item or elsewhere (as for locally filmed videos), make up a title and put brackets around it in the 245 field. Add a 500 note that says: **Title supplied by cataloger.** When cataloging a multi-part item, use the guide or container as the Chief Source of Information if this is the only source of a collective title.

Title (MARC field 245 ‡a and ‡b)

Use the title from the Chief Source of Information as the Title Proper (245 ‡a) and Other Title Information (245 ‡b; usually subtitle). Notice whether the 245 title varies from the title on the video label, front or spine of container, guide, or in the distributor's catalog. If so, make a 500 note about each variant title, such as **Title on cassette label: Title.** Trace title variants in 246 fields if the difference is in the first five words. Also in a 246 field, trace the subtitle or other portion of the title if someone might think that is the title. Before format integration in 1995, variant titles were traced in 740 fields. Older MARC records in large databases may trace such variants in 740 fields. These 740 fields should be changed to 246 fields.

General Material Designation (GMD) (MARC field 245 ‡h)

For a videocassette, videotape reel, or videodisc, the GMD is **[videorecording]**. Use a 538 note for type of videocassette. A ½ in. cassette is VHS or Beta (becoming obsolete), and a ¾ in. videocassette is U-matic. For a VHS videocassette (most ½ inch videocassettes currently sold), the 538 note will say **VHS format.** For a ¾ inch videocassette, the 538 note will say **U-matic format.** For a videodisc, use a 538 note such as **CLV format** only if this information appears on the videodisc.

Interactive Video Programs

Rules for cataloging interactive video programs are still evolving. Early interactive video programs consisted of a videodisc with accompanying computer floppy disk(s), used with VCR and computer linked. Catalogers did not agree on whether to catalog these sets as videodiscs with accompanying software, as computer programs, or as kits. Later, Level III videodiscs had both video and computer components on the same disc.

Because of catalogers' confusion in determining whether these items should be cataloged as video programs or as computer software, a few years ago OLAC (Online Audiovisual Catalogers, Inc.) successfully requested a new GMD for interactive video: **[interactive multimedia]**. However, this new GMD does not appear in AACR2R, 2nd ed., 1998 revision. The GMD **[interactive multimedia]** was approved as an experimental GMD for use in OCLC records for U.S. libraries. A change of GMD is under consideration, but **[interactive multimedia]** should be used for interactive video programs until a change is official. The new GMD is expected to be **[electronic resource]**.

A videodisc does not qualify as interactive multimedia just because its guide or container <u>says</u> it is interactive. To determine whether a videodisc is truly interactive multimedia, use *Guidelines for Bibliographic Description of Interactive Multimedia*. Some videodiscs may say "interactive" because they come with a barcode directory. A barcode directory is a booklet or list of barcodes used with a barcode reader to directly access specific chapters or subject locations in the video program. Such videodiscs are <u>not</u> interactive multimedia. To qualify as interactive multimedia, the videodisc should say Level III or higher on it, <u>or</u> it should come with accompanying computer software (video player and computer are connected and used simultaneously). If there is any doubt about whether a videodisc meets the criteria for interactive multimedia, it should be cataloged using GMD **[videorecording]**.

Statement of Responsibility (245 ‡c)

Cataloging records for AV items often have several Statements of Responsibility in 245 ‡c, joined by semicolons, such as the <u>production company</u> or other company responsible for the contents of the program, <u>writer</u>, <u>producer</u>, and <u>director</u>. In general, other persons responsible for the program go in the 508 Credits Note, not in 245 ‡c, in the following order, separated by space-semicolon-space: executive producers ; director of photography or cameramen ; editors ; composers of background music.

Production companies can be transcribed in 245 ‡c, but should be put in a 500 note (before responsible persons) if their statement of function on the item would make a lengthy statement of responsibility. In practice, AV catalogers may put production companies either in 245 ‡c or in a 500 note. Always put them in a 500 note if their statement of function is found outside the Chief Source of Information, such as on the container or in a guide.

Statements of function in 245 ‡c should be copied exactly as given on the Chief Source of Information. For example, if the program says **written, directed & produced by Kevin Brownlow & David Gill**, put this phrase in the Statement of Responsibility exactly as it appears on the video, including ampersands (&). If the program says **written by Kevin Brownlow & David Gill, directed by Kevin Brownlow & David Gill, produced by Kevin Brownlow & David Gill**, the rules do not allow the cataloger to combine these into one statement in 245 ‡c as in the first example. List them exactly as they appear, separated by space-semicolon-space. Such exact transcription is a basic principle for 245 ‡c when cataloging any format. However, in the 508 Credits Note, statements of function are <u>not</u> copied exactly and usually should not contain the word **by**. For example, if the video credits say **edited by John Smith**, the 508 will say **editor, John Jones** or **editing, John Jones**.

Publisher/Distributor (260 ‡a and ‡b)

The publisher of a videocassette may or may not be the same as the company that produced it. If these are two different companies, put the production company in the Statement of Responsibility (if it is found on the Chief Source of Information) or in a 500 note if preferred. Put the publishing company in 260 ‡b. Occasionally a video is jointly published by two companies and each should appear in 260 (‡a and ‡b are repeatable). Repeated ‡a and ‡b are also used when a distributor is stated on the item or the cataloger wishes to include a distributor not stated on the item. See p. 7 in Chapter 1 for examples. Always trace the production company of a video. In addition, most catalogers also trace the publisher and a distributor that is stated on the item. Some catalogers trace bracketed distributors (not stated on the item); others do not trace bracketed distributors.

Date (260 ‡c)

The 260 ‡c is usually the copyright date of the video program. The copyright date is usually at the beginning or end of the program. If the copyright date does not appear on the program, it may appear on the label of the videocassette or videodisc. The container may have a later copyright date, but that is usually for the container design, not for the video program itself. If there is a conflict, infer the copyright date on the container as the publication date and use both dates in the date area (260 ‡c). Bracket the publication date without c preceding the actual copyright date (e.g., ‡c [1990], c1986.).

Occasionally a video program will have two conflicting copyright dates on the program itself, either one at the beginning and one at the end, or both at the end. This often happens with TV programs, movies published in video format, and sound filmstrips or slide programs reissued on video. The earlier copyright is usually for the original program, and the later copyright is usually for the video version. AACR2R and LC rule interpretations are unclear on how to handle the 260 ‡c in such cases where the format has changed but the contents have not. Catalogers may handle the date in one of two ways depending on individual rule interpretation.

One interpretation of the rules on date is that since the video version represents a change in format, the date area should contain only the copyright of the video version, and the original program copyright should be in a 500 note. However, microform reproductions of books are also a change in format, but catalogers do not use the date of the microform reproduction in 260 ‡c. Instead, they use the original date (the date of the contents), in 260 ‡c with a note giving date of reproduction. Following this line of reasoning, some video catalogers interpret cataloging rules on date to mean that since the true copyright of the program contents is the earlier copyright, this date should be transcribed as the copyright date in 260 ‡c. Catalogers who take this position on date add the later copyright date (the copyright date of the video version) in brackets as the publication date without c, as for other video programs published in a later year than copyrighted. The inferred and bracketed publication date precedes the original program copyright date in 260 ‡c. Then both dates appear on screen indexes in online catalogs, not just the copyright date of the video version, which may mislead users about the date of the program contents. Online indexes extract dates from 260 ‡c.

Here are two examples of the date dilemma for video programs. For example, the unchanged 1998 video version of a 1980 sound filmstrip will still have 1980 contents, and **c1998** (copyright of video version) on the public index screen will make the patron believe the information is recent. Likewise, a video version of a TV program on Russia actually produced and copyrighted in 1990 (shortly before the end of Communist rule) and reissued on video in 1996 would be very different from a program on Russia produced in 1996. If **c1996** (copyright of the later video version) appears on the online catalog's index screen rather than **[1996], c1990** (inferred publication date from video version copyright, and copyright of original program contents), the library patron will assume from the date **c1996** that this program is about the reorganized Russia.

In practice, AV catalogers are entering these conflicting copyright dates both ways: either the copyright of the video version in 260 ‡c with a note about the original copyright of the program; or both dates in 260 ‡c with the copyright of the video version as inferred publication date in brackets before the original copyright of the program contents. To add further confusion, sometimes it is not clear whether a video program was originally a television program or not, so the cataloger may be uncertain about whether this is actually a different format or a program published after it was copyrighted. This date dilemma seems to be a cataloger's judgment call, depending on individual interpretation of the rules and what the cataloger wants the patron to see on the index screen.

Physical Description Area (MARC field 300)

See AACR2R, Chapter 7, for examples of the Physical Description Area for videocassettes, videodiscs, and motion pictures.

If there is more than one videocassette or videodisc on the cataloging record, the running time will be the total of all. If all are the same length, the running time of each can be given, as in the third example below. Examples:

    300   **‡a 1 videocassette (30 min.) : ‡b sd., col. ; ‡c ½ in.**

    300   **‡a 3 videocassettes (88 min.) : ‡b sd., col. ; ‡c ½ in.**

    300   **‡a 3 videocassettes (30 min. each) : ‡b sd., col. ; ‡c ½ in.**

If there are two or more separately-titled, independent programs on a videocassette or videodisc with a collective title on its label, use the label title as the Title Proper and catalog the item as one unit. Give the total running time in the Physical Description Area (300 ‡a). Add a Contents Note (505 field) with part-titles and running times of the separate parts (see example, p. 57).

If there are separately-titled, independent programs on a videocassette or disc with <u>no</u> collective title on its label, each program may be cataloged separately. The Extent of Item (300 ‡a) for each separately-cataloged program on one videocassette should be such as the following: **on 1 videocassette (30 min.).** Another cataloging option would be to put the separate program titles in 245 separated by space-semicolon-space. The first program title would be in 245 ‡a followed by the GMD in ‡h, space-semicolon-space, ‡b, and the other program title(s) separated by space-semicolon-space.

Other Physical Details (300 ‡b) indicates sound or silent, and color or black-and-white or a combination. Most videos have a sound track. Old silent movies on video may have an added music background but will still be designated as **sd.** The only time **si.** Is used is when <u>no</u> sound is present at all, as for original versions of old silent movies (no music sound track). If the video is in color with some black-and-white, record this in 300 ‡b as **col. With b&w sequences** (see example, p. 52). If there is about an even mix of both, record this as **col. And b&w** or **b&w and col.**, depending on which seems to predominate.

Dimensions (300 ‡c) are the width of the videotape (½ inch for VHS and Beta, ¾ inch for U-matic). For VHS and Beta videocassettes, record ½ in. in the Dimensions area (300 ‡c). For U-matic videocassettes, record ¾ in. The Dimensions area for videodiscs contains the diameter of the disc (usually **12 in.**). Accompanying materials are added in a single 300 ‡e, as for other formats.

Series

The series title may be given on the program itself (often before the title frame on the program) or on the video label, container, or in accompanying printed material. Record this title in a 440 field unless the series is prominent enough to put in the Title Proper area (245 ‡a), followed by ‡n and ‡p, then ‡h. Example:

> **245 00 ‡a Five centuries of music in Venice. ‡n Program 1, ‡p Venice and the Gabrielis ‡h [videorecording] / ‡c created by H.C. Robbins Landon ; producers, Jillian Robinson, Tony Sutcliffe ; director, Hilary Boulding.**

Usually, however, a series title will appear in a 440 field (i.e., traced in this form). If the series title could go in a 440 field but the official traced form is not identical to the series title as given on the item, transcribe the series title from the item in a 490 field with first indicator 1, and trace the official form of the series title in 830. Number designations in 440, 490, or 830 are entered in ‡v.

Notes (MARC fields 5XX)

Here are some common 5XX notes for videos. There are others. See AACR2R and Chapter 1-2 of this book for more notes. Follow the order of notes described as follows.

> **•Format Note (538 field)**
> For a videocassette, this note tells whether the video is VHS, Beta, or U-matic (e.g., **VHS format.**). For videodiscs, it tells whether the disc is CLV or CAV (used only if stated on the item).

> **•Language Note (546 field)**
> If the video is closed-captioned, audio-described, in a foreign language, or in sign language, put this information in a 546 note. For example:
> **Closed-captioned and audio-described.**
> **In French with English subtitles.**
> **In American Sign Language with narration.**

> **•Source of Title Note (500 field)**
> If there is no title frame, and the Title Proper comes from another source (usually the label on the videocassette or videodisc), add a 500 note stating where the 245 title came from.

- **Variant Title Note (500 field)**

  Titles on label, container, guide, and in the distributor's catalog may vary. Put these variations in 500 notes so that they can be traced in 246 fields.

- **Statement of Responsibility Note: Corporate Body (500 field)**

  If a corporate body has responsibility for the contents and does not appear in 245 ‡c, describe the function of the corporate body in a 500 note. Some catalogers occasionally name and trace the copyright holder if it differs from the publisher, assuming that this corporate body may have some responsibility for the contents. Other catalogers always ignore the copyright holder. This is a case-by-case judgment call.

- **Statement of Responsibility Note: Cast (511 field)**

  A 511 Cast Note may be used for dramatic productions (musical or nonmusical). First indicator 1 generates the print constant **Cast:**.

- **Statement of Responsibility Note: Performer (511 field)**

  A 511 General Performer Note is used for host, narrator, speakers, or for performers of music. First indicator 0 does not generate a print constant.

- **Statement of Responsibility Note: Credits (508 field)**

  Most videos name some or all of the following: executive producers, directors of photography (or cameramen), editors, composers of music. These persons should be listed in the 508 Credits Note. If writers, producers, and directors are found outside the Chief Source of Information, they are listed in the Credits Note instead of in 245 ‡c. Occasionally there will be <u>no</u> 508 Credits Note because these responsible persons are not in the program credits. Generates the print constant **Credits:** on the public screen.

- **Edition/History of Publication Note (500 field)**

  Needed if AV item was originally in another format or based on another work. Examples:
  Originally produced as a motion picture in 1992.
  Based on the novel by John Steinbeck.

- **Date/Place of Recording Note (518 field)**

  If information is readily available, tell when/where the program was recorded, or tell when it was taped off-air. Examples:
  Recorded in Mar. 1983 at Momaday's home in Tucson, Ariz.
  Recorded live at the Eisenhower Theater, Kennedy Center for the Performing Arts.
  Taped off-air with permission, Sept. 5, 1998.

- **Physical Description Note (500 field)**

  Provides information that cannot be given in the 300 field, or information about a change in physical format. Examples:
  Videocassette version of a segment from the PBS television series, Nova.
  Videocassette version of a 1960 motion picture released by Metro-Goldwyn-Mayer.
  Stills with narration. Videocassette version of a 1981 sound filmstrip released by Educational Filmstrips.

•**Audience Note (521 field)**

Use only if this information is stated on video, container, or accompanying printed material. Examples:

MPAA rating: PG-13.

For primary grades.

•**Summary Note (520 field)**

A video program always needs a 520 Summary Note. Be objective and concise, but include enough detail that the patron can tell what the program is about. Include terms for keyword searching. Generates the print constant **Summary:**.

•**Contents Note (505 field)**

Include a Contents Note if the videocassettes or videodiscs in a set (or segments on one cassette or disc) have separate titles, and put the running time of each in parentheses after the part-title. A 505 Contents Note can also be used to show running times for numbered parts without part-titles. Generates print constant **Contents:**.

•**Awards Note (586 field)**

If information about awards is readily available, add an Awards Note. A blank first indicator generates the print constant **Awards:**. Examples of 586 text:

Academy Award for Best Picture, 1962.

Academy Award for Best Song (A whole new world [Aladdin's theme]), Alan Menken and Tim Rice; and Academy Award for Best Score, Alan Menken.

Cine Golden Eagle; Golden Venus.

Subject Headings and Added Entries (MARC fields 6XX and 7XX)

For closed-captioned videos, the Sears subject heading is **Closed caption video recordings** (equivalent to the 650 Library of Congress subject heading, **Video recordings for the hearing impaired**). Sears does not yet have a subject heading for audio-described videos, so the LC subject heading, **Video recordings for the visually handicapped**, may be borrowed. However, keep in mind that a future Sears heading for audio-described videos may be patterned after the Sears heading for closed-captioned videos, and thus may be Audio described video recordings. Sears does not have a subject heading for open-captioned videos, but LC uses the same subject heading as for closed-captioned videos, **Video recordings for the hearing impaired**. If Sears adds a subject heading for open-captioned videos, it may follow the same pattern as the subject heading for closed-captioned videos, such as Open caption video recordings.

For full-length motion pictures (over 60 min.), use the 650 LC subject heading, **Feature films**. Sears does not have a similar generic subject heading. For fiction-type films under 60 min., Sears and LC both use the 650 subject heading, **Short films**. In both LC and Sears are subject headings for specific types of films such as **Documentary films**, **Horror films**, **Western films**, **Musical films**, etc. See Chapter 1 for information about other subject headings and added entries.

Copy Cataloging of Video Formats

If the library receives catalog cards or MARC records from AV distributors along with new video titles, or uses cataloging records from a shared database as a basis for the local cataloging record, these cataloging records should be checked very carefully. Some cataloging records may be prepared from data sheets without the video in hand, or the cataloger may have cataloged the video from eye-readable data without putting it in a viewer to see beginning and ending credits. Some important information may be missing or inaccurate. Some cataloging records from distributors are prepared in a nonstandard way, by non-catalogers.

The 245 title on cataloging records from large databases or AV companies may be the video label title rather than the title frame title. On video formats, the title often varies. The Chief Source of Information is the program itself. Cataloging information should be transcribed from the video label only when the needed information is not on the viewed program. Some catalogers are not careful about accounting for variant titles. Look on label, front and spine of container, guide, and in the distributor's catalog to see if any of these titles vary from the Chief Source of Information. If so, add appropriate 500 notes and 246 title tracings. On older cataloging records, some of these variant titles may appear in 740 fields rather than in 246 fields and should be re-tagged.

The Statement of Responsibility in 245 ‡c may be incomplete or incorrect (e.g. transcribed from back of container, not from program itself). It may be recorded in 511 or 508 fields rather than 245 ‡c. Information on responsible persons may even be missing altogether.

The place and publisher for the 260 field may be correct because these often appear on the video label or container. But the date on cataloging records from other sources may be a problem if the cataloger did not look at the program. Often the copyright date of the program is in the end credits. The cataloger may have accepted the eye-readable copyright date on cassette label or container as the date of the program contents, but this date may actually be the date of the label or container design and not the date of the program.

The running time in the 300 field may be incorrect or missing from the cataloging record, and this is very important for videos used in the classroom. Harking back to earlier cataloging rules, the physical description may include **(VHS)** before the running time in 300 ‡a, rather than a 538 note, **VHS format**.

The series (440 field) may be missing or incorrect, especially if the series title differs on program and eye-readable portions of the item. The series program number may be missing.

If present, the 538 note (e.g., **VHS format.**) may not be listed first and/or may be tagged 500. Now cataloging practice places the 538 format note <u>first</u> rather than as a Physical Description Note placed later in the sequence of notes.

The cataloger may have missed the closed captions, especially if the **CC** symbol is not prominent on the video and the program was not viewed using equipment with a closed-caption feature. A 546 note must be added: **Closed-captioned**. Also add a 650 subject heading for this feature.

Statement of Responsibility notes about corporate bodies (500 fields), performers or cast (511 notes), or persons with technical responsibility (508 Credits Note) may be missing because this information was in the credits of the program and the cataloger did not put the video in a viewer. The 520 Summary Note may be missing, sketchy, or copied directly from the distributor's catalog (which tends toward sales pitch rather than objective information about the program). Nearly always the 520 Summary Note will need to be rewritten or expanded for good keyword access. The 505 Contents Note may be missing (or may lack running times) for multi-part videos.

Subject access may be inadequate. Subject headings may be Library of Congress, not Sears. Important responsible persons and corporate bodies may not be traced. The basis for some 7XX tracings may not appear in the descriptive cataloging portion of the cataloging record. Some access points may be in incorrect form.

Question everything when using cataloging records from other sources to create the local record. Much editing will probably be needed.

Processing Video Formats

Videocassettes often come in colorful cardboard containers that may contain much information about the program, including some cataloging information not found anywhere else. Purchase plastic videocassette containers that open like a book and have a plastic "sleeve" around them. Cut the cardboard container apart and slip it into the plastic sleeve for an attractive container that provides program information and preserves cataloging data.

Educational video programs often come with guides. If a guide will fit in the video container, store it there so that it will be readily available for users. For economy of space, some libraries keep larger guides and accompanying printed materials in a file separate from the video shelves. But when a patron checks out a videorecording, the guide might be forgotten. Attach a strip to the video label and container saying **Guide available**.

If both the videorecording and accompanying printed items come in a commercial container intended for shelving, keep the set in this container if possible. Discarded containers may have variant titles or important descriptive information. If the eye-readable title differs from the title on the title frame, attach a strip to the item stating the 245 field title to eliminate confusion when items are checked in and out.

Examples of cataloging records for video formats follow.

Example of documentary video program:

245 00   ‡a Long shadows ‡h [videorecording] / ‡c produced, directed, narrated by Ross Spears ; co-writer, Jamie Ross.

246 3   ‡a Long shadows : ‡b the legacy of the American Civil War

246 3   ‡a Legacy of the American Civil War

260   ‡a Johnson City, TN : ‡b James Agee Film Project, ‡c c1987.

300   ‡a 1 videocassette (89 min.) : ‡b sd., col. With b&w sequences ; ‡c 1/2 in.

538   ‡a VHS format.

500   ‡a Title on container: Long shadows : the legacy of the American Civil War.

508   ‡a Cinematography, Anthony Forma, Neil Means, Nancy Schreiber ; editors, Neil Means, Ross Spears, Grahame Weinbren ; music, Kenton Coe.

520   ‡a Uses interviews and archival footage to explore ways in which the Civil War can still be felt in American society: from politics to economics, from civil rights to foreign policy, from individual to collective memory, from South to North to West. With comments from C. Vann Woodward, John Hope Franklin, Robert Penn Warren, Studs Terkel, Tom Wicker, Jimmy Carter, Albert Murray, Virginius Dabney, and others. Features weekend soldiers, blues singers, battlefield guides, relic collectors, West Pointers, Vietnam veterans, former movie stars, and Civil Rights activists.

651 8   ‡a United States ‡x History ‡y 1861-1865, Civil War.

651 8   ‡a Southern States.

651 8   ‡a Documentary films.

700 1   ‡a Spears, Ross.

700 1   ‡a Ross, Jamie.

710 2   ‡a James Agee Film Project.

Note: There are some differences in the way cataloging information is transcribed on catalog cards and MARC records. In this example, note that the 508 and 520 fields do not include the first word on the catalog card in that field. Most systems supply <u>print constants</u> (**Credits:** for 508 and **Summary:** for 520) for those fields on the public screen. The added title entries in the tracings paragraph of the catalog card are relocated on the MARC record to 246 fields, without the beginning word <u>Title</u>. Initial articles are not used in MARC title fields except in 245. In 6XX fields on the MARC record there are no dashes as on the catalog card. For subject headings on the public screen, library systems supply dashes in place of 6XX ‡v, ‡x, ‡y, and ‡z. Also, dashes are not entered on MARC records between fields such as Statement of Responsibility and Place of Publication.

Catalog card version:

Long shadows [videorecording] / produced, directed, narrated by Ross Spears ; co-writer, Jamie Ross. -- Johnson City, TN : James Agee Film Project, c1987.
     1 videocassette (89 min.) : sd., col. with b&w sequences ; ½ in.

VHS format.
    Title on container: Long shadows : the legacy of the American Civil War.
    Credits: Cinematography, Anthony Forma, Neil Means, Nancy Schreiber ; editors, Neil Means, Ross Spears, Grahame Weinbren ; music, Kenton Coe.

 (Continued on next card)

Long shadows [videorecording] ... c1987.   (Card 2)

   Summary: Uses interviews and archival footage to explore ways in which the Civil War can still be felt in American society from politics to economics, from civil rights to foreign policy, from individual to collective memory, from South to North to West. With comments from C. Vann Woodward, John Hope Franklin, Robert Penn Warren, Studs Terkel, Tom Wicker, Jimmy Carter, Albert Murray, Virginius Dabney, and others. Features weekend soldiers, blues singers, battlefield guides, relic collectors, West Pointers, Vietnam veterans, former movie stars, and civil rights activists.

 (Continued on next card)

Long shadows [videorecording] ... c1987.   (Card 3)

    1. United States--History--1861,1865, Civil War. 2. Southern States. 3. Documentary films. I. Spears, Ross. II. Ross, Jamie. III. James Agee Film Project. IV. Title: Long shadows : the legacy of the American Civil War. V. Title: The legacy of the American Civil War.

Example of documentary video program:

028 40   ‡a FFH 5863 245 00 ‡b Films for the Humanities & Sciences

245 00   ‡a Altered states ‡h [videorecording] : ‡b a history of drug use in America / ‡c producer, Ann Spurling.

246 30   ‡a History of drug use in America

260   ‡a Princeton, N.J. : ‡b Films for the Humanities & Sciences, ‡c [1996], c1993.

300   ‡a 1 videocassette (58 min.) : ‡b sd., col. With b&w sequences ; ‡c ½ in.

538   ‡a VHS format.

500   ‡a A production of WXXI-TV in conjunction with the Strong Museum exhibition: Altered states / curated by Patricia Tice.

511 0   ‡a Narrator, William J. Pearce.

508   ‡a Videographer, Doug Steffer ; editor, Michael Conolly.

500   ‡a Original copyright date on program, c1993. Copyright of video version, c1996. Date on container, c1995.

520   ‡a A documentary on drug use and abuse in America, from the days when the early European settlers became enamored with tobacco, through Prohibition, and up to the present. Reasons for substance abuse have remained constant: to ease pain, alleviate boredom, or to expand the consciousness. Documents the cultural, social, and political movements that impacted, or were impacted by, the use of drugs. Includes tobacco, alcohol, caffeine, opium, cocaine, LSD, marijuana and other substances. Shows that drug use is not a contemporary phenomenon or problem but has been a constant presence throughout the country's social history.

650 8   ‡a Drug abuse ‡x History.

650 8   ‡a Alcoholism ‡x History.

650 8   ‡a Tobacco habit ‡x History.

650 8   ‡a Documentary films.

700 1   ‡a Spurling, Ann.

700 1   ‡a Tice, Patricia M., ‡d 1953-

710 2   ‡a Films for the Humanities (Firm)

710 2   ‡a WXXI (Television station : Rochester, N.Y.)

710 2   ‡a Margaret Woodbury Strong Museum.

Example of an award-winning documentary video program that was originally a motion picture and later a television program. Date on cassette label is apparently erroneous.

028 40 ‡a 4077 ‡b Gateway Films/Vision Video

245 04 ‡a The Amish ‡h [videorecording] : ‡b a people of preservation / ‡c written and produced by John L. Ruth.

246 30 ‡a People of preservation

260 ‡a Worcester, PA : ‡b Gateway Films/Vision Video, ‡c c1996.

300 ‡a 1 videocassette (53 min.) : ‡b sd., col. ; ‡c ½ in.

538 ‡a VHS format.

500 ‡a Produced by Heritage Productions.

511 0 ‡a Narrators, John L. Ruth, Harley Wagler, John A. Hostetler.

508 ‡a Executive producer, Hiram Hershey ; camera, Burton Buller ; editor, Nicholas Spies.

500 ‡a Date on cassette label, c1991. Date on program, c1996.

500 ‡a Videocassette version of a 1975 motion picture. PBS documentary featured on the television series, 60 minutes.

518 ‡a "Filmed in Lancaster County, Pennsylvania--the oldest Amish community in America"--container.

520 ‡a Examines the history, values, beliefs and way of life of the Old Order Amish, a "people of preservation" who coexist with modern society but who do not allow technology to change their way of life. Stresses the importance of simplicity and community in Amish life. Shows Amish people farming, playing, attending school, and conducting business. Explains the difference between the Amish and the Mennonites.

586 ‡a Cine Golden Eagle ; Golden Venus.

650 8 ‡a Amish ‡x Social life and customs.

650 8 ‡a Documentary films.

700 1 ‡a Ruth, John L.

710 2 ‡a Gateway Films.

710 2 ‡a Vision Video (Firm)

710 2 ‡a Heritage Productions.

730 0 ‡a 60 minutes (Television program)

Example of an educational video:

028 40	‡a 824B ‡b InService Video Network
245 00	‡a Dealing with diversity in the classroom ‡h [videorecording] / ‡c presenter, Kenneth J. Doka ; producer, Mark Abney.
260	‡a Livingston, NJ : ‡b InService Video Network, National Association of Secondary School Principals, ‡c [1993], c1992.
300	‡a 1 videocassette (26 min.) : ‡b sd., col. ; ‡c ½ in.
538	‡a VHS format.
500	‡a Presented by Instructivision, Inc. and the National Association of Secondary Schools Principals.
500	‡a Executive producer, Jay Comras ; editor, Andy Abbot.
500	‡a Running time on cassette label, 22 min. Actual running time, 26 min.
521 8	‡a "For teachers, administrators, parents, students"--container.
520	‡a Examines how to effectively teach, motivate, and evaluate culturally diverse student populations. Explains how demographic changes have affected the goals of education and have shifted policy from "melting pot" assimilation to cultural pluralism. Discusses why student behavior should be interpreted with care and explains how to organize a classroom and curriculum to make all students feel welcome and equal.
650 8	‡a Multicultural education.
650 8	‡a Teaching.
650 8	‡a Race relations.
700 1	‡a Doka, Kenneth J.
700 1	‡a Abney, Mark.
710 2	‡a InService Video Network.
710 2	‡a National Association of Secondary School Principals (U.S.)
710 2	‡a Instructivision, Inc.

Example of instructional video, originally four motion pictures, now all on one video with collective title. Third and fourth part-titles vary on container.

028 40	‡a 113C ‡b National Film Board of Canada
245 00	‡a Path of the paddle ‡h [videorecording] / ‡c director, Bill Mason ; producer, Bill Brind.
260	‡a [New York] : ‡b National Film Board of Canada, ‡c [1990], c1977.
300	‡a 1 videocassette (112 min.) : ‡b sd., col. ; ‡c 1/2 in.
538	‡a VHS format.
500	‡a Third and fourth part-titles listed on container as: Double basic ; Double whitewater.
511 0	‡a Canoeists, Bill Mason, Paul Mason ; commentary, Bill Mason.
508	‡a Executive producer, Colin Low ; photography, Ken Buck ; editor, Bill Mason ; music, Larry Crosley.
500	‡a Originally issued as four motion pictures in 1977.
500	‡a Program notes on container.
520	‡a Four programs on the techniques of safe canoeing. First program demonstrates basic strokes for controlling the canoe, with animated lines showing what the paddle is doing. Second program explains how to locate a deep-water channel, and tells how to guide the canoe through rapids and how to survive a wipeout. Third program shows how to apply basic paddling strokes. Last program shows how to read the rapids, plan a course, and control the canoe with all the basic paddling strokes.
505 0	‡a Solo basic (28 min.) -- Solo whitewater (28 min.) -- Doubles basic (28 min.) -- Doubles whitewater (28 min.).
650 8	‡a Canoes and canoeing.
700 1	‡a Mason, Bill, ‡d 1929-
700 1	‡a Brind, Bill.
700 1	‡a Mason, Paul.
710 2	‡a National Film Board of Canada.
740 02	‡a Solo basic.
740 02	‡a Solo whitewater.
740 02	‡a Doubles basic.
740 02	‡a Doubles whitewater.
740 02	‡a Double basic.
740 02	‡a Double whitewater.

Example of a videodisc containing two separate travel programs, with collective title on label. Programs were previously published as separate videocassettes. Spelling Macao is official LC form for subject heading. Credits were checked in a videodisc player.

020	‡a 0929756681
245 00	‡a Hong Kong, Macau & Singapore ‡h [videorecording].
246 3	‡a Hong Kong, Macau and Singapore
246 3	‡a Hong Kong and Macau
260	‡a San Ramon, Calif. : ‡b International Video Network ; ‡a Louisville, KY : ‡b Ztek Co. [distributor], ‡c c1990.
300	‡a 1 videodisc (56 min.) : ‡b sd., col. ; ‡c 12 in.
440 0	‡a Video visits. ‡p Far East collection
538	‡a CLV format. Recorded on one side only.
500	‡a Title from disc label.
500	‡a Title in distributor's catalog: Hong Kong and Macau.
500	‡a Part-titles on container: Hong Kong & Macau ; Singapore.
511 0	‡a Narrator of first program, Jane St. Claire ; narrator of second program, Bruce Robertson.
508	‡a First program: producers/directors, Patrick Sun, James Omi ; script, Patrick Sun, James Cramer ; camera, Michael Heumann, Susan Heumann ; editor, Michael Heumann ; music, Ric Halsted, Dave Packer. Second program: producer/director, Michael Heumann ; writers, Larry Habegger, Michael Heumann ; camera/editing, Michael Heumann, Susan Heumann ; music, Radhika Miller, Reed Maidenberg.
500	‡a Previously issued as two videocassette programs, c1986 and c1988.
500	‡a Copyright of program 1 held by Video Postcard Souvenirs, Ltd. Copyright of program 2 held by Sonoma Video, Santa Rosa, Calif.
500	‡a Program notes on container.
520	‡a The first program visits folk theatre performances, street markets, department stores, and other places in Hong Kong. Shows outer islands with their fishing villages and monasteries. Travels through the New Territories via the Kowloon Canton Railway. Visits Macau, a Portuguese colony and the oldest settlement in Asia. The second program visits landmarks in Singapore including the Padang, Parliament House, Cricket Club, Raffles Hotel, Temple of Heavenly Happiness, Sultan Mosque, Sri Mariamman, Newton's Circus, Orchard Road, and Sentosa Island.
505 0	‡a Impressions of Hong Kong and Macau (25 min.) -- Singapore, crossroads of Asia (31 min.).
651 8	‡a Hong Kong (China) ‡x Description.
651 8	‡a Macao ‡x Description.
651 8	‡a Singapore ‡x Description.
700 1	‡a Sun, Patrick.
700 1	‡a Omi, James.

700 1   ‡a Cramer, James.
700 1   ‡a Heumann, Michael.
700 1   ‡a Habegger, Larry.
710 2   ‡a International Video Network.
710 2   ‡a Ztek Co.
710 2   ‡a Video Postcard Souvenirs, Ltd.
710 2   ‡a Sonoma Video Productions.
740 02   ‡a Impressions of Hong Kong and Macau.
740 02   ‡a Singapore, crossroads of Asia.
740 02   ‡a Hong Kong & Macau.
740 02   ‡a Singapore.

Example of closed-captioned feature film on video. Sears does not have a subject heading equivalent to the LC subject heading, Feature films**.**

028 40   ‡a M902693 ‡b MGM/UA Home Video

245 00   ‡a Of mice and men ‡h [videorecording] / ‡c Metro-Goldwyn-Mayer ; a Russ Smith/Gary Sinise production ; screenplay by Horton Foote ; produced by Russ Smith and Gary Sinise ; directed by Gary Sinise.

260   ‡a [Culver City, Calif.] : ‡b MGM/UA Home Video ; ‡a [Itasca, Ill. : ‡b Distributed by Critics' Choice Video, ‡c 1993], c1992.

300   ‡a 1 videocassette (113 min.) : ‡b sd., col. ; ‡c 1/2 in.

538   ‡a VHS format. Hi-fi Dolby surround stereo.

546   ‡a Closed-captioned.

511 1   ‡a John Malkovich, Gary Sinise, Casey Siemaszko, Ray Walston, Sherilyn Fenn, Alexis Arquette, Joe Morton, Richard Riehle, John Terry, Noble Willingham.

511 0   ‡a Music orchestrated and conducted by Ken Kugler.

508   ‡a Executive producer, Alan C. Blomquist ; director of photography, Kenneth MacMillan ; editor, Robert L. Sinise ; music, Mark Isham.

500   ‡a Copyright held by MGM-Pathe Communications Co.

500   ‡a Based on the novel by John Steinbeck.

500   ‡a Originally produced as a motion picture in 1992.

518   ‡a Filmed on location in the Santa Ynez Valley and Los Angeles, Calif.

521 8   ‡a MPAA rating: PG-13.

520   ‡a In Depression-era California, two migrant workers dream of better days on a spread of their own until an act of unintentional violence leads to tragic consequences.

650 0   ‡a Feature films.

600 18   ‡a Steinbeck, John, ‡d 1902-1968 ‡v Film and video adaptations.

650 8   ‡a Closed caption video recordings.

700 1   ‡a Smith, Russell E.

700 1   ‡a Sinise, Gary.

700 1   ‡a Foote, Horton.

700 1   ‡a Malkovich, John.

700 1   ‡a Siemaszko, Casey.

700 1   ‡a Walston, Ray, ‡d 1917-

700 1   ‡a Fenn, Sherilyn.

700 1   ‡a Isham, Mark.

700 1   ‡a Steinbeck, John, ‡d 1902-1968.

710 2   ‡a Metro-Goldwyn-Mayer.

710 2   ‡a MGM/UA Home Video (Firm)

710 2   ‡a Critics' Choice Video.

710 2   ‡a MGM-Pathe Communications Co.

Example of a filmed play produced for television. Some important credits were not found on the Chief Source of Information and are in the 508 Credits Note.

028 40   ‡a 69936 ‡b LIVE Home Video

245 00   ‡a Antony and Cleopatra ‡h [videorecording] / ‡c by William Shakespeare ; directed for television by Jon Scoffield.

246 3   ‡a Antony & Cleopatra

246 3   ‡a William Shakespeare's Antony & Cleopatra

246 3   ‡a William Shakespeare's Antony and Cleopatra

260   ‡a Van Nuys, Calif. : ‡b LIVE Home Video ; ‡a [Itasca, Ill. : ‡b Distributed by Critics' Choice Video, ‡c 1993], c1974.

300   ‡a 1 videocassette (161 min.) : ‡b sd., col. with b&w sequences ; ‡c 1/2 in.

440 0   ‡a Literary masterpieces

538   ‡a VHS format. Hi-fi.

500   ‡a Title on cassette label: Antony & Cleopatra.

500   ‡a Title on container: William Shakespeare's Antony & Cleopatra.

500   ‡a Presented by ITC Entertainment Group. Copyright held by ATV Network Ltd.

511 1   ‡a Richard Johnson (Antony), Janet Suzman (Cleopatra), Corin Redgrave (Octavius Caesar), Patrick Stewart (Emobarbus) ; Royal Shakespeare Company.

508   ‡a Executive producer for television, Cecil Clarke ; staged for television by Trevor Nunn ; producer, Cecil Clarke ; music, Guy Woolfenden.

500   ‡a Video version of the 1974 television production.

520   ‡a Television movie based on Shakespeare's drama of Mark Antony's obsessive passion for Queen Cleopatra, and how it leads to the tragic downfall of both.

650 0   ‡a Feature films.

600 18   ‡a Antonius, Marcus, ‡d 83?-30 B.C. ‡v Drama.

600 08   ‡a Cleopatra, ‡c Queen of Egypt, ‡d d. 30 B.C. ‡v Drama.

600 18   ‡a Shakespeare, William, ‡d 1564-1616 ‡v Film and video adaptations.

700 1   ‡a Shakespeare, William, ‡d 1564-1616.

700 1   ‡a Scoffield, Jon.

700 1   ‡a Johnson, Richard, ‡d 1927-

700 1   ‡a Suzman, Janet.

700 1   ‡a Redgrave, Corin.

700 1   ‡a Stewart, Patrick, ‡d 1940-

700 1   ‡a Clarke, Cecil.

700 1   ‡a Nunn, Trevor.

700 1	‡a Woolfenden, Guy.
710 2	‡a LIVE Home Video (Firm)
710 2	‡a Critics' Choice Video.
710 2	‡a ITC Entertainment Group.
710 2	‡a ATV Network Ltd.
710 2	‡a Royal Shakespeare Company.

Example of a videodisc version of a classic motion picture. It is not identical to the original release but has been altered somewhat. Opening credits were checked. It was not possible to get to end credits without letting the program run in its entirety, so end credits were not checked.

020	‡a 0782000169
028 40	‡a LV25551 ‡b Republic Pictures Home Video
245 00	‡a Macbeth ‡h [videorecording] / ‡c by William Shakespeare ; directed by Orson Welles.
250	‡a 45th anniversary ed.
260	‡a [Los Angeles, Calif.] : ‡b Republic Pictures Home Video, ‡c c1992.
300	‡a 1 videodisc (112 min.) : ‡b sd., b&w ; ‡c 12 in.
538	‡a CLV format. Extended play.
500	‡a "Restored by UCLA Film Archives and the Folger Shakespeare Library, Washington, D.C."
500	‡a "Charles K. Feldman presents a Mercury production by Orson Welles."
511 1	‡a Orson Welles (Macbeth), Jeanette Nolan (Lady Macbeth), Dan O'Herlihy (Macduff), Roddy McDowall (Malcolm), Edgar Barrier (Banquo), Alan Napier (a Holy Father).
508	‡a Director of photography, John L. Russell ; editor, Louis Lindsay ; music, Jacques Ibert ; conductor, Efrem Kurtz.
500	‡a Videodisc release of the 1948 motion picture restored to its pre-release length in 1980.
500	‡a Date of videodisc version from disc label. Date in opening credits, c1948.
520	‡a Original, fully restored Republic Pictures production of Shakespeare's Macbeth, directed by Orson Welles. Restoration replaces the long cut (over 20 min.) removed before original release, and features the version of the soundtrack in which the characters speak with Scottish accents. Shot in 21 days and considered to be one of the greatest experimental films ever made under the Hollywood studio system. In Shakespeare's classic story of murder, witchcraft, and revenge, Macbeth, driven by overwhelming ambition and an unscrupulous wife, murders the King of Scotland and claims the throne for himself. He begins a violent reign of terror and execution in a desperate attempt to maintain his power. Haunted by ghosts and vexed by witches, he and his wife rapidly descend into the depths of madness and paranoia as the weight of their crimes proves their undoing.
650 0	‡a Feature films.
650 8	‡a Experimental films.
600 8	‡a Shakespeare, William, ‡d 1564-1616 ‡v Film and video adaptations.
700 1	‡a Shakespeare, William, ‡d 1564-1616.
700 1	‡a Welles, Orson, ‡d 1915-
700 1	‡a Feldman, Charles K., ‡d 1904-1968.
700 1	‡a Nolan, Jeanette, ‡d 1911-
700 1	‡a O'Herlihy, Dan, ‡d 1919-
700 1	‡a McDowall, Roddy.

700 1   ‡a Barrier, Edgar, ‡d 1907-1964.

700 1   ‡a Napier, Alan, ‡d 1903-

700 1   ‡a Ibert, Jacques, ‡d 1890-1962.

710 2   ‡a Republic Pictures Home Video (Firm)

710 2   ‡a University of California, Los Angeles. ‡b Film Archives.

710 2   ‡a Folger Shakespeare Library.

710 2   ‡a Mercury Productions.

710 2   ‡a Republic Pictures Corporation.

Example of a children's animated feature film on video with closed-captioning and audio description. Sears does not have subject headings Children's films **or** Feature films.

020	‡a 1558906630
028 40	‡a 1662 ‡b Walt Disney Home Video
245 00	‡a Aladdin ‡h [videorecording] / ‡c Walt Disney Pictures ; co-produced by Donald W. Ernst ; screenplay by Ron Clements and John Musker, Ted Elliott and Terry Rossio ; produced and directed by John Musker, Ron Clements ; co-producer, Amy Pell.
260	‡a Burbank CA : ‡b Walt Disney Home Video ; ‡a Boston, MA : ‡b DVS Home Video, ‡c [1994?], c1992.
300	‡a 1 videocassette (92 min.) : ‡b sd., col. ; ‡c ½ in.
440 0	‡a Walt Disney classics
538	‡a VHS format. Dolby hi-fi stereo.
546	‡a Closed-captioned and audio-described.
511 0	‡a Voices, Scott Weinger (Aladdin), Robin Williams (Genie), Linda Larkin (Jasmine), Jonathan Freeman (Jafar), Frank Welker (Abu), Randy Cartwright (carpet), Gilbert Gottfried (Iago), Douglas Seale (Sultan) ; audio description, Nancy Baker.
508	‡a Co-producers, Donald W. Ernst, Amy Pell ; editor, H. Lee Peterson ; music, Alan Menken, Howard Ashman, Tim Rice.
500	‡a Videocassette release of the 1992 animated motion picture, with added closed-captioning and audio description.
521 8	‡a MPAA rating: G.
520	‡a Set in the mythical city of Agrabah, the story follows a street-smart peasant, Aladdin, and his mischievous pet monkey, Abu. Aladdin falls in love with the free-spirited Princess Jasmine, despite a law that says she must wed a royal suitor. His luck changes with one rub of the lamp, releasing the shape-shifting, fun-loving, wish-giving Genie, who turns him into a Prince. But the evil sorcerer Jafar and his wisecracking parrot Iago also crave the lamp's power. If Aladdin is to defeat them and win Jasmine's heart, he must learn to be himself, and that is one wish the Genie cannot grant.
586	‡a Academy Award for Best Song (A whole new world [Aladdin's theme]), Alan Menken and Tim Rice; and Academy Award for Best Score, Alan Menken.
650 8	‡a Animated films.
650 8	‡a Musical films.
650 0	‡a Feature films.
650 0	‡a Children's films.
650 8	‡a Closed caption video recordings.
650 0	‡a Video recordings for the visually handicapped.
700 1	‡a Ernst, Donald W.
700 1	‡a Clements, Ron.
700 1	‡a Musker, John.

700 1   ‡a Elliott, Ted.

700 1   ‡a Rossio, Terry.

700 1   ‡a Pell, Amy.

700 1   ‡a Williams, Robin, ‡d 1952 July 21-

700 1   ‡a Menken, Alan.

700 1   ‡a Ashman, Howard.

700 1   ‡a Rice, Tim.

710 2   ‡a Walt Disney Pictures.

710 2   ‡a Walt Disney Home Video (Firm)

710 2   ‡a DVS Home Video (Firm)

Example of a children's liveaction feature film on video with several variant titles in 246 fields. Liveaction is not usually specifically noted, but is added to this 520 Summary Note since one might expect a Dr. Seuss film to be animated.

028 40 ‡a 90163 ‡b RCA/Columbia Pictures Home Video

245 04 ‡a The 5000 fingers of Dr. T ‡h [videorecording] / ‡c screenplay by Dr. Seuss, Allan Scott ; directed by Roy Rowland.

246 3 ‡a Five thousand fingers of Dr. T

246 3 ‡a Dr. Suess's The 5000 fingers of Dr. T

246 3 ‡a Dr. Seuss's The five thousand fingers of Doctor T

246 3 ‡a Doctor Seuss's The 5000 fingers of Dr. T

246 3 ‡a Doctor Seuss's The five thousand fingers of Dr. T

260 ‡a Burbank, Calif. : ‡b RCA/Columbia Pictures Home Video, ‡c [1991], c1953.

300 ‡a 1 videocassette (92 min.) : ‡b sd., col. ; ‡c ½ in.

538 ‡a VHS format.

500 ‡a Title on cassette label: Dr. Seuss's The 5000 fingers of Dr. T.

500 ‡a A Stanley Kramer Company production. Presented by Columbia Pictures Corp.

511 1 ‡a Peter Lind Hayes, Mary Healy, Hans Conried, Tommy Rettig, John Heasley, Noel Cravat.

508 ‡a Producer, Stanley Kramer ; director of photography, Frank Planer ; editor, Al Clark ; music, Frederick Hollander ; lyrics, Dr. Seuss ; choreography, Eugene Loring.

500 ‡a Preceded by an advertising segment (ca. 3 min.), not included in running time.

520 ‡a Young Bart Collins dreams of his piano teacher, Dr. Terwilliker. Dr. T wants to prove that his method of teaching piano is the best method in the world. He banishes all other musical instruments and lures 500 boys to perform on the biggest grand piano ever built. Liveaction.

650 0 ‡a Children's films.

650 8 ‡a Fantasy films.

650 0 ‡a Feature films.

700 1 ‡a Seuss, ‡c Dr.

700 1 ‡a Scott, Allan, ‡d 1907-

700 1 ‡a Rowland, Roy.

700 1 ‡a Kramer, Stanley.

700 1 ‡a Hayes, Peter Lind, ‡d 1915-

700 1 ‡a Healy, Mary, ‡a 1918-

700 1 ‡a Conried, Hans.

700 1 ‡a Rettig, Tommy, ‡d 1941-

700 1 ‡a Hollaender, Friedrich.

700 1   ‡a Loring, Eugene, ‡d 1914-

710 2   ‡a RCA/Columbia Pictures Home Video.

710 2   ‡a Stanley Kramer Company.

710 2   ‡a Columbia Pictures Corporation.

Example of a video version of a three-part sound filmstrip. There are two publishers and various other corporate bodies with responsibility for the contents. The only date on the item is for the original filmstrip.

028 40   ‡a 0-676-27445-5 ‡b American School Publishers

245 00   ‡a Greece ‡h [videorecording] / ‡c written by Gordon Bensley ; produced by John Dent & Cal Industries for Educational Enrichment Materials.

260   ‡a [Westminster, Md.] : ‡b Random House Video ; ‡a [Hightstown, N.J.] : ‡b American School Publishers, ‡c [199-?], c1979.

300   ‡a 1 videocassette (37 min.) : ‡b sd., col. ; ‡c ½ in. + ‡e 1 teacher's guide (1 folded sheet).

490 1   ‡a Western man and the modern world

538   ‡a VHS format.

500   ‡a Copyright held by Pergamon Press, Inc.

500   ‡a Based on the textbook series, Western man and the modern world, published by Pergamon Press, 1979.

500   ‡a Stills with narration. Videocassette version of a sound filmstrip.

520   ‡a Looks at ancient Greece in terms of the relationship of history and philosophy to art, with emphasis on significant artistic achievements as a result of key historical or philosophical events. Sees early Greek history in the light of the Homeric epics. Observes the architecture of the Acropolis in relation to the philosophy of Pythagoras. Illustrates the Greek love of independence using both modern and historical examples. Shows that art expresses the fundamental ideas of a civilization's concept of life. Pt. 1 summarizes early Archaic history, touching on Homer, Agamemnon, Ulysses, Solon, and archeologist Schliemann; also gives a rapid survey of several pre-Classical philosophers, concentrating on the Pythagorean concept of numbers. Pt. 2 explores the twin concepts of independence and unity, central to the Greek way of life, and elaborates in a historical context with an anecdotal narration on the Persian Wars. Pt. 3 touches on the Classical Era as a result of the Persian Wars and focuses on the special relationship between thought and art in Classical Greece.

505 0   ‡a pt. 1 (11 min.) -- pt. 2 (9 min.) -- pt. 3 (17 min.).

650 8   ‡a Greece ‡x Civilization.

651 8   ‡a Greece ‡x Antiquities.

651 8   ‡a Classical antiquities.

651 8   ‡a Greek art.

651 8   ‡a Greek architecture.

700 1   ‡a Bensley, Gordon.

700 1   ‡a Dent, John.

710 2   ‡a Cal Industries.

710 2   ‡a Educational Enrichment Materials, inc.

710 2   ‡a Random House Video.

710 2   ‡a American School Publishers.

710 2   ‡a Pergamon Press, Inc.

830 0   ‡a Western man and the modern world (Westminster, Md.)

Example of one part of a video series cataloged separately, entered under series title followed by part-title (no volume number present). Cataloged under collective title with 505 Contents Note listing parts.

020	‡a 1562195166
028 40	‡a CPM 1516 ‡b Central Park Media
245 00	‡a This great century. ‡p 1900-1918, a new world/beyond the front ‡h [videorecording] / ‡c screenplay, Jean-Paul Thomas ; director, Pierre Philippe.
246 30	‡a 1900-1918, a new world/beyond the front
246 30	‡a New world/beyond the front
246 3	‡a Our century
260	‡a New York, N.Y. : ‡b Central Park Media Corp., ‡c [1996], c1990.
300	‡a 1 videocassette (109 min.) : ‡b sd., b&w with col. sequences ; ‡c ½ in.
538	‡a VHS format.
500	‡a Title from cassette label.
500	‡a Produced by Cinematheque Gaumont and Vision 7.
511 0	‡a Narrator, Mike Marshall.
508	‡a Editors, Annick Bruell, Christine Keller ; music, Robert Viger.
500	‡a Series previously published as: Our century.
500	‡a Preceded by brief advertising segment (4 min.), not included in running time.
520	‡a First in a five-part series that surveys historical events of the 20th century, using original newsreels and vintage footage. Covers major advances, trends, and tragedies, from political upheavals and passing social crazes to the role of technology, and examines their impacts on the future. This segment documents world events from 1900 to 1900, including the Titanic, Marie Curie, World War I, and Charlie Chaplin.
505 0	‡a 1900/1914, a new world (54 min.) -- 1914/1918, beyond the front (55 min.).
650 8	‡a Modern history ‡y 1900-1999 (20th century)
650 8	‡a United States ‡x History ‡y 1900-1999 (20th century)
650 8	‡a Twentieth century.
650 8	‡a Europe ‡x History ‡y 1900-1999 (20th century)
650 8	‡a World War, 1914-1918.
610 28	‡a Titanic (Steamship)
600 18	‡a Curie, Marie, ‡d 1867-1934.
600 18	‡a Chaplin, Charlie, ‡d 1889-1977.
700 1	‡a Thomas, Jean-Paul.
700 1	‡a Philippe, Pierre.
700 1	‡a Marshall, Mike.

710 2 ‡a Central Park Media (Firm)

710 2 ‡a Gaumont (Firm)

710 2 ‡a Vision 7 (Firm)

740 02 ‡a 1900/1914, a new world.

740 02 ‡a New world.

740 02 ‡a 1914/1918, beyond the front.

740 02 ‡a Beyond the front.

Example of one part of a video series cataloged separately (series title in 245 ‡a). No part-title on item. Cataloging information is from eye-readable labels. Components are described in a 505 Contents Note. No numbers on unit guides (order of unit guides from content guide for series).

020	‡a 1564602206 (Unit guide 1)
020	‡a 1564602214 (Unit guide 2)
020	‡a 1564602222 (Unit guide 3)
020	‡a 1564602230 (Unit guide 4)
020	‡a 1564602249 (Unit guide 5)
020	‡a 1564602257 (Unit guide 6)
020	‡a 1564602265 (Unit guide 7)
020	‡a 1564602907 (Print directory)
245 00	‡a Life science. ‡n Volume 2 ‡h [videorecording].
260	‡a Warren, NJ : ‡b Optical Data Corp., ‡c [1994], c1989.
300	‡a 1 videodisc : ‡b sd., col. ; ‡c 12 in. + ‡e 11 booklets.
538	‡a Laser optical CAV format. Stereo option.
546	‡a Audio in English and Spanish.
500	‡a Title from disc label.
508	‡a Authors, Elizabeth R. Paxton, Theodore T. May, Anne Marie Muhlhauser ; program developers, William E. Clark, Elizabeth R. Paxton ; program design, Elizabeth R. Paxton … [et al.] ; videodisc production, Stephanie Petron Cahill.
500	‡a Ed. on unit guides: 1st barcode ed.
500	‡a Date on videodisc, c1989. Date on booklets, c1994.
521 8	‡a For grades 4 through 8.
520	‡a Interactive video lessons in life science, designed for classroom use. Each lesson contains pictures, diagrams, movie clips and activities.
505 0	‡a Videodisc -- Unit guide [1]. Introducing the human body (xv, 66 p. ; 28 cm.) -- Unit guide [2]. The body outside in : skin, muscles, bones, joints, care (xv, 105 p. ; 28 cm.) -- Unit guide [3]. Don't get nervous : nervous system, senses (xv, 121 p. ; 28 cm.) -- Unit guide [4]. Breathe easy : respiratory system, gas exchange, care (xv, 68 p. ; 28 cm.) -- Unit guide [5]. The heart of the matter : circulatory system, gas exchange, care (xv, 101 p. ; 28 cm.) -- Unit guide [6]. You are what you eat : digestive system, food groups, nutrients (xv, 89 p. ; 28 cm.) -- Unit guide [7]. Life goes on : asexual and sexual reproduction, life cycles, genetics (xv, 95 p. ; 28 cm.) -- Content guide for series (44 p. ; 28 cm.) -- Print directory of barcodes for visuals (92 p. ; 28 cm.) -- Teacher resources manual for series (32 p. : col. ill. ; 28 cm.) -- Technology guide (1 tri-folded sheet ; 28 cm.).
650 8	‡a Human anatomy ‡x Study and teaching.
650 8	‡a Physiology ‡x Study and teaching.

700 1	‡a Paxton, Elizabeth R.
700 1	‡a May, Theodore T.
700 1	‡a Muhlhauser, Anne Marie.
700 1	‡a Clark, William E.
700 1	‡a Cahill, Stephanie Petron.
710 2	‡a Optical Data Corporation.
740 02	‡a Introducing the human body.
740 02	‡a Body outside in.
740 02	‡a Don't get nervous.
740 02	‡a Breathe easy.
740 02	‡a Heart of the matter.
740 02	‡a You are what you eat.
740 02	‡a Life goes on.

Example of a multi-part video program, cataloged as a set. No part-titles. Identical durations. Fourth subject heading subdivision borrowed from the Library of Congress.

028 40   ‡a UPRF101--UPRF105 ‡b Adult Learning Service

245 00   ‡a Upon reflection ‡h [videorecording] : ‡b ethnicity and race / ‡c producer, Marcia Alvar ; director, Cynthia Halterman.

246 30   ‡a Ethnicity and race

260   ‡a [Alexandria, Va.] : ‡b PBS Adult Learning Service, ‡c c1996-1997.

300   ‡a 5 videocassettes (30 min. each) : ‡b sd., col. ; ‡c ½ in.

538   ‡a VHS format.

500   ‡a Subtitle from cassette label.

500   ‡a Presented by UWTV. Produced by University News & Information, University of Washington, UWTV video production.

511 0   ‡a Host, Marcia Alvar ; guests, Jonathan Kaufman (episode 101, Feb. 20, 1997), Morris Dees (episode 102, Jan. 14, 1997), Tetsuden Kashima (episode 103, Apr. 3, 1997), Ellis Cose (episode 104, Jan. 24, 1997), Samuel DeWitt Proctor (episode 105, Mar. 1, 1996).

508   ‡a Executive producer, Jack N. Armstrong ; camera, Celeste Glende ... [et al.] ; editor, David Ris ; music, Antonio Vivaldi.

520   ‡a Marcia Alvar, University of Washington, discusses race and ethnicity issues with five guests. The first episode features Jonathan Kaufman, author of A hole in the heart of the world, which follows the lives of several generations of Jews from Eastern Europe who find a renewed faith and pride as they uncover their heritage, buried first by the Nazis and later by the Communists. The second episode features Morris Dees, director and chief counsel for the Southern Poverty Law Center, who pioneered the legal strategy that holds racists groups financially accountable for the violent actions of their followers. The third episode features Tetsuden Kashima, who studied the relocation of Japanese and Japanese American citizens that occurred on the West Coast during World War II, a time when racial prejudice and fear upset the delicate balance between the rights of a citizen and the power of the state. The fourth episode features Ellis Cose, author of Color Blind, contributing editor for Newsweek, who explores the question of whether a truly race-neutral society is possible. The fifth episode features Samuel DeWitt Proctor, theologian, educator, and civil rights activist, who chronicles his own life against the whole of black progress and discusses how it is possible to overcome ongoing prejudice and deceptive racial stereotypes. Proctor, grandson of slaves, served in the administrations of Presidents Kennedy and Johnson, and served as teacher and advisor to such leaders as Martin Luther King, Jr., and Jesse Jackson.

650 8   ‡a Race.

650 8   ‡a Jews ‡z Europe ‡x History.

650 8   ‡a World War, 1939-1945 ‡z Europe.

650 8   ‡a Japanese Americans ‡x Evacuation and relocation, 1942-1945.

650 8   ‡a World War, 1939-1945 ‡z United States.

650 8   ‡a African Americans ‡x Civil rights ‡x History.

700 1   ‡a Alvar, Marcia.

700	1	‡a Halterman, Cynthia.
700	1	‡a Kaufman, Jonathan.
700	1	‡a Dees, Morris.
700	1	‡a Kashima, Tetsuden.
700	1	‡a Cose, Ellis.
700	1	‡a Proctor, Samuel D.
710	2	‡a PBS Adult Learning Service.
710	2	‡a University of Washington.
710	2	‡a UWTV (Television station : Seattle, Wash.)

Example of a video version of a two-part sound filmstrip. Original filmstrip credits and date are not on video version. A liveaction introduction has been added. Two subject headings were borrowed from the Library of Congress.

028 40   ‡a 7VH 0053 ‡b Clearvue/eav

245 00   ‡a Impressionism in art and music ‡h [videorecording].

260   ‡a Chicago, IL : ‡a Clearvue/eav, ‡c c1986.

300   ‡a 1 videocassette (34 min.) : ‡b sd., col. with b&w sequences ; ‡c ½ in. + ‡e 1 booklet of program notes (19 p. ; 28 cm.) + 3 worksheet masters with instructions (4 leaves).

538   ‡a VHS format.

500   ‡a Mostly stills with narration. Videocassette version of a 1970 filmstrip from Educational Audio Visual, with added liveaction introduction by Roya Megnot.

500   ‡a Booklet of program notes includes script.

520   ‡a Draws parallels between art's use of color and light and music's use of instrumentation, while examining Impressionist themes. Examines the centrality of nature, Asian influences, and the break with traditional forms. Discusses the Impressionist movement as a precursor to 20th-century developments. Discusses the works of Monet, Pissarro, Ravel, Debussy, and others. Pt. 1 outlines the basic principles of Impressionism as practiced by Monet and Debussy. Pt. 2 extends the discussion to other artists and composers.

505 0   ‡a [Introduction] (3 min.) -- pt. 1. Monet and Debussy (17 min.) -- pt. 2. The influence of Impressionism (14 min.).

650 0   ‡a Art and music.

650 0   ‡a Impressionism (Music)

650 8   ‡a Impressionism (Art)

600 18   ‡a Monet, Claude, ‡d 1840-1926.

600 18   ‡a Debussy, Claude, ‡d 1862-1918.

600 18   ‡a Pissarro, Camille, ‡d 1830-1903.

600 18   ‡a Ravel, Maurice, ‡d 1875-1937.

700 1   ‡a Megnot, Roya.

710 2   ‡a CLEARVUE/eav (Firm)

710 2   ‡a Educational Audio Visual, Inc.

740 02   ‡a Monet and Debussy.

740 02   ‡a Influence of Impressionism.

Example of an instructional video with open captions (there is no appropriate Sears subject heading):

245 00		‡a I see what you're saying ‡h [videorecording] : ‡b a practical guide to speechreading / ‡c created by Karen Webb for New York League for the Hard of Hearing ; producers, Michael Tuomey, Bob Marty ; director, Bob Marty ; writers, Esther Miller Beckoff ... [et al.].
246 30		‡a Practical guide to speechreading
246 3		‡a I see what you are saying
260		‡a New York, N.Y. : ‡b New York League for the Hard of Hearing, ‡c c1990.
300		‡a 2 videocassettes (177 min.) : ‡b sd., col. ; ‡c ½ in. + ‡e 1 guide for vol. 1 (26 p. ; 18 cm.) + 1 guide for vol. 2 (6 p. ; 18 cm.).
538		‡a VHS format.
546		‡a Open captioned.
500		‡a A production of MPI, Media Productions International, Inc., New York.
511 0		‡a Hosts, Karen Webb, Paul W. Smith ; featuring Gene Wilder ; players, George Harris, Melody James, Marti Raim ; readers, Esther Miller Beckoff ... [et al.].
508		‡a Executive producer, Karen Webb ; camera, Frank Lombardo, Bill Rosser ; editors, Bob Marty, Michael Tuomey ; music, Walter Raim.
520		‡a Demonstrates techniques of speechreading. It is more than watching other people's lips move; it means understanding the speaker through a combination of seeing, hearing and thinking techniques. Includes a series of lessons, dialogue, and skits. Demonstrations are by Gene Wilder and members of the New York League for the Hard of Hearing. To provide practice in speechreading, speech samples have been altered electronically so that the words are unintelligible.
505 0		‡a vol. 1. Fundamentals (109 min.) -- vol. 2. Practice (68 min.).
650	8	‡a Deaf ‡x Means of communication.
650	8	‡a Deaf ‡x Education.
700 1		‡a Webb, Karen.
700 1		‡a Tuomey, Michael.
700 1		‡a Marty, Bob.
700 1		‡a Beckoff, Esther Miller.
700 1		‡a Smith, Paul W.
700 1		‡a Wilder, Gene, ‡d 1935-
710 2		‡a New York League for the Hard of Hearing.
710 2		‡a Media Productions International, Inc.

Example of a lecture, with personal author main entry. Part of a set with no part-titles, cataloged separately.

028 40   ‡a 8001 ‡b Quality Educational Media

100 1   ‡a Glasser, William, ‡d 1925-

245 10   ‡a Glasser on relationships. ‡n Part 1 ‡h [videorecording] / ‡c produced and directed by Jim Thompson.

246 3   ‡a Relationships, the core of good teaching

246 3   ‡a Core of good teaching

260   ‡a San Pedro, CA : ‡b Quality Educational Media, Inc., ‡c c1997.

300   ‡a 1 videocassette (29 min.) : ‡b sd., col. ; ‡c ½ in.

538   ‡a VHS format.

500   ‡a Title in distributor's catalog: Relationships : the core of good teaching.

500   ‡a A presentation of Jim Thompson Productions, Inc., in association with Naylor-Barber, Inc.

508   ‡a Photographer/editor, Wayne Threm.

520   ‡a Part of a series in which Dr. William Glasser presents his newest ideas about relationships and how they affect student behavior and academic achievement. This segment explores the challenge of developing better relationships; the significance of making enormous progress in technology but not in human relationships; why positive relationships are critical to success in schools, homes, and workplaces; the negative effects of stimulus-response psychology; and his ideas on a more effective psychology of relationships.

650 8   ‡a Human relations.

650 8   ‡a Teacher-student relationships.

650 8   ‡a Teaching.

650 8   ‡a Educational psychology.

700 1   ‡a Thompson, Jim.

710 2   ‡a Quality Educational Media, Inc.

710 2   ‡a Jim Thompson Productions, Inc.

710 2   ‡a Naylor-Barber, Inc.

Example of a locally recorded video program (originally a slide program). Subject headings are based on a Library of Congress subject heading but place names can be added in Sears. Subject subdivisions are from Sears.

245 02 ‡a A taste of sassafras ‡h [videorecording] / ‡c Southwest Missouri State University Media Productions.

260 ‡c 1990.

300 ‡a 1 videocassette (25 min.) : ‡b sd., col. with b&w sequences ; ‡c ½ in.

538 ‡a VHS format.

500 ‡a Stills with narration. Video version of a sound slide program.

518 ‡a Dubbed with permission at Southwest Missouri State University, 1990.

520 ‡a Overview of the Ozarks region: physical features, natural resources, industries, mining, people and places.

651 8 ‡a Ozark Mountains Region ‡x Description.

651 8 ‡a Ozark Mountains Region ‡x Social life and customs.

710 2 ‡a Southwest Missouri State University. ‡b Media Productions Dept.

NOTES

CHAPTER 4
CATALOGING FILMSTRIPS AND SLIDES

Narrated filmstrip and slide programs have mostly given way to video formats. Some filmstrips and slides with sound cassettes are still available for purchase, but most are several years old. Filmstrips and slide programs may be reissued in videocassette format, with the same still pictures and original sound track. They are then cataloged as videos. Silent slide programs in such fields as art and botany are still available, usually with a printed booklet or slide list describing each slide for the teacher to use in presenting the material in the classroom. School libraries doing retrospective conversion may need to catalog sound filmstrips, silent filmstrips, and slide sets already in their collections. However, these older materials should be evaluated for possible weeding, or replacement with a video version if available.

AACR2R Rules for Filmstrips and Slides

Use the cataloging rules in AACR2R Chapter 8. These rules sometimes refer back to general rules in AACR2R Chapter 1, or to rules in AACR2R Chapter 7 (used for videos). Cataloging filmstrips or slides is very similar to cataloging videos, except for the GMD (245 ‡h), Physical Description Area (300 field), and some 5XX notes.

Previewing

Filmstrips and slide sets may be silent, or they may have a separate sound track. Sound programs should be previewed and timed. Sound cassettes that accompany filmstrips or slide programs often have audible signals (beeps) on one side of the cassette and inaudible signals on the other side. The side with inaudible signals is intended to be used in a combination projector and cassette player that advances the filmstrip or slide carousel automatically, triggered by the inaudible signals on the cassette. Sometimes both sides of the cassette are identical, with both audible and inaudible signals. For filmstrips in a series, the sound cassettes may have the sound tracks of two programs on one cassette (one on each side) with both audible and inaudible signals on each side.

Some filmstrips or slide sets already in the collection from years past may have the sound track on a 12-inch LP record, but these should be considered for weeding. They will have to be played in two separate pieces of equipment (filmstrip projector and record player) and advanced manually.

If automatic equipment is available for classroom use to project a filmstrip or slide set with accompanying sound cassette, use the automatic side of the cassette to preview and time the program. Make sure the visuals and sound are synchronized. Occasionally a sound track omits an inaudible signal or there are extra inaudible signals. Try another projector to be sure that the problem is not in the previewing equipment. If there are problems with synchronization for a newly purchased program, contact the distributor. Most distributors will provide a replacement cassette. However, the missing inaudible signal(s) or extra inaudible signal(s) may be on the master, and the replacement may be just like the original. Older sound filmstrips and slide programs may also have synchronization problems, and replacement may not be possible. If a cassette with faulty inaudible signals cannot be replaced, make a note in the script where the problem occurs so that the projectionist can adjust manually, or caution users to play only the side of the cassette with audible signals.

There will not be a digital timer on the previewing equipment for these formats. The program must be timed with a stop watch. Time sound filmstrips and slide sets using the same principle as timing videos. Do not start the stop watch when the cassette player is turned on; but wait until sound is heard. Usually the running time in 300 ‡e will be only <u>one</u> side of the cassette, which is the time it will take to run the program in the classroom. This is true when one side of the cassette has the sound track with inaudible signals, and the other side has audible signals for use with manual equipment. If the tape must be turned over to finish viewing the program, the running time will be the duration of both sides.

If the cataloger is also the previewer of the entire filmstrip program, before running the program in its entirety, roll manually through the opening credits and title frame to transcribe cataloging information. Back up to the frame that directs viewers to start the sound track, start the sound, and time the program with a stop watch. At the end of the program, let the sound track finish and turn off the stop watch. Then reverse the filmstrip manually to look for other cataloging information in the end credits. It is not a good idea to stop and start the sound filmstrip program and stop watch while trying to transcribe credits. It is easy to forget to stop or start the stop watch and to fail to get an accurate running time. If a previewer times the program, the cataloger usually needs to see only beginning and ending credits. A small silent filmstrip viewer is adequate for the cataloger to view credits, unless there is no script or written description and it is necessary to hear some of the narration to write a 520 Summary Note.

Chief Source and Prescribed Sources of Information

The Chief Source of Information and the Prescribed Sources are listed in AACR2R Chapter 8. The Chief Source of Information will usually be the title frame, other opening credits, and ending credits, as for videocassettes. If there is no title frame for a slide set, but the title is printed on the slide mounts, consider the slide mount as the substitute Chief Source of Information. If neither the projected program nor the slide mounts contain information needed for the 245 field, or there is no title frame for a filmstrip, choose a substitute Chief Source of Information from the following (in this order): container; accompanying textual material such as a guide; or other sources, such as distributor's catalog. Always make a 500 Source of Title Note if the source is other than the projected program.

GMD (245 ‡h)

For a filmstrip, the GMD is **[filmstrip]**. For a slide set, the GMD is **[slide]** (not [slide set] or [slides]).

Physical Description Area (300 field)

Examples of the Physical Description Area are found in AACR2R Chapter 8. The number of frames for a filmstrip will appear in parentheses in 300 ‡a in the same position as the running time for a video. Slides will appear as the number of slides. Examples:

300   **‡a 1 filmstrip (45 fr.)**
300   **‡a 45 slides**

Hold a filmstrip by its edges and pull it through the fingers to count the number of filmstrip frames, starting with the first <u>content</u> frame after the focus frame(s). This may or may not be the title frame. Do not count the end frame if it is preceded by several blank frames, which usually means that the automatic advance will stop advancing the filmstrip before the end frame appears on the screen. To wind the filmstrip back into a roll to put it back in its container, start small. Do not pull to make the roll smaller, because this will cause vertical scratch lines ("cinch marks") from dust particles on the film.

Slides are like filmstrips cut apart with frames mounted separately. Count all slides. Slides load in the slide carousel with the picture upside down (projects right side up). Most slide sets have numbers on the slide mounts. Most are inserted into the slide carousel by holding the numbered corner between thumb and forefinger. The slide numbers are then visible to the projectionist in the carousel tray. If the slide number does not serve as the "thumb mark" for loading the slides, there may be a dot on one corner of each slide mount that is meant to be at upper right when inserting the slide. Some slide sets do not have a thumb mark on the slides, and the pictures may be turned various ways when slides are loaded with the slide number at upper right. If the user is likely to be confused about how to load the slides into the slide carousel, use a small-tipped magic marker to add dots to the slide mounts at upper right loading position to serve as thumb marks. This will save the user much frustration. Some libraries purchase small, sticky colored dots to place on slide mounts as thumb marks, but these can come off during handling or projection.

The running time does not go in 300 ‡a as for videos. The sound track for a filmstrip or slide set is an accompanying item and goes in 300 ‡e, followed by its running time in parentheses. For 300 ‡b, Other Physical Details, record only **col.** or **b&w** or a combination. For 300 ‡c, dimensions of filmstrips are usually **35 mm.** For slides, do not give dimensions unless the slides are a nonstandard size (standard is 2 x 2 in.). Add accompanying sound cassette and guide in 300 ‡e using plus signs.

Here are examples of the Physical Description Area (300 field) for a filmstrip with cassette and an identical slide set with cassette:

300 **‡a 1 filmstrip (45 fr.) : ‡b col. ; ‡c 35 mm. + ‡e 1 sound cassette (15 min.) + 1 guide (35 p. ; 28 cm.).**

300 **‡a 45 slides : ‡b col. + ‡e 1 sound cassette (15 min.) + 1 guide (35 p. ; 28 cm.).**

Occasionally a set of filmstrips has a sound track with <u>both</u> manual and automatic signals on the same side of the sound cassette, and each side of the cassette has the sound track for a <u>different</u> filmstrip (e.g., a set of four filmstrips with two cassettes). If each of these filmstrips is cataloged separately, the 300 field for a single filmstrip will be such as the following:

300 **‡a 1 filmstrip (45 fr.) : ‡b col. ; ‡c 35 mm. + ‡e 1 side of 1 sound cassette (15 min.) + 1 guide (25 p. ; 19 cm.).**

For a filmstrip or slide set with a script and no sound, the 300 field will be as follows:

300 **‡a 1 filmstrip (45 fr.) : ‡b col. ; ‡c 35 mm. + ‡e 1 script (12 p. ; 19 cm.).**

300 **‡a 45 slides : ‡b col. + ‡e 1 script (12 p. ; 19 cm.).**

Notes (5XX fields)

As for videos, filmstrips and slides will need a 508 Credits Note if persons with the appropriate technical roles are stated on the filmstrip or in the guide. For a sound filmstrip or slide set, catalogers use a standard physical description note to show that the sound track has both audible and inaudible signals:

> **500   ‡a Sound accompaniment compatible for manual and automatic operation.**

If the sound track has only audible or only inaudible signals, use only the appropriate term so that the user can tell what kind of equipment is necessary.

Filmstrips and slides need a 520 Summary Note. For a set of two or more parts, add a 505 Contents Note with individual part numbers and part-titles. Put the number of filmstrip frames or slides and the running time in parentheses after the part-titles.

Subject Headings and Added Entries (6XX and 7XX fields)

See general guidelines for AV formats in Chapter 1.

Examples follow.

Example of a filmstrip with sound cassette, entered under the series title with ‡n and ‡p in the 245 field.

245 00 ‡a Dangerous dieting, the wrong way to lose weight. ‡n Part 3, ‡p Eating disorders ‡h [filmstrip] / ‡c written and produced by Ray Messecar.

246 30 ‡a Wrong way to lose weight

246 30 ‡a Eating disorders

260 ‡a Pleasantville, N.Y. : ‡b Human Relations Media, ‡c c1983.

300 ‡a 1 filmstrip (78 fr.) : ‡b col. ; ‡c 35 mm. + ‡e 1 sound cassette (22 min.) + 1 series guide (57 p. ; 21 cm.).

508 ‡a Photographers, Mieke Maas ... [et al.].

500 ‡a Sound accompaniment compatible for manual and automatic operation.

504 ‡a Series guide includes script, discussion questions, and bibliographical references (p. 24).

520 ‡a Briefly examines social pressures which have contributed to society's dangerous obsession with thinness. Explores causes and effects of eating disorders, especially anorexia nervosa and bulimia among young women. Also tells about a young man obsessed with exercising to keep his weight down. Tells possible ways to treat patients with eating disorders.

650 8 ‡a Anorexia nervosa.

650 8 ‡a Bulimia.

650 8 ‡a Eating disorders.

650 8 ‡a Weight loss.

700 1 ‡a Messecar, Ray.

710 2 ‡a Human Relations Media, inc.

Example of a filmstrip with sound cassette. This sound track is in both English and Spanish. One subject heading is Library of Congress because there is no corresponding Sears subject heading.

245 02	‡a A classroom with blocks ‡h [filmstrip] / ‡c script, Terry Tyor, Jean Berlfein.
260	‡a Washington, D.C. : ‡b National Association for the Education of Young Children, ‡c c1979.
300	‡a 1 filmstrip (86 fr.) : ‡b col. ; ‡c 35 mm. + ‡e 1 sound cassette (English narration, 13 min. ; Spanish narration, 15 min.).
546	‡a Narration in English and Spanish. On each side of the cassette, the English narration is followed by the Spanish narration.
511 0	‡a Narration, Diana Munatones.
508	‡a Photography, Jean Berlfein.
500	‡a Based on: The block book / Elizabeth S. Hirsch, editor.
500	‡a Sound accompaniment compatible for manual and automatic operation.
520	‡a Shows ways preschool and early elementary children can use blocks for both playing and learning. Describes skills children learn by using blocks, such as building maps and models. Stresses the value of play as a learning experience.
650 8	‡a Preschool education.
650 8	‡a Elementary education.
650 0	‡a Block building (Education)
650 8	‡a Play.
700 1	‡a Berlfein, Jean.
700 1	‡a Tyor, Terry.
710 2	‡a National Association for the Education of Young Children.
740 0	‡a Block book.

Catalog card version:

A classroom with blocks [filmstrip] / script, Terry Tyor, Jean Berlfein.
-- Washington, D.C. : National Association for the Education of
Young Children, c1979.
    1 filmstrip (86 fr.) : col. ; 35 mm. + 1 sound cassette (English
narration, 13 min. ; Spanish narration, 15 min.).

Narration in English and Spanish. On each side of the cassette, the
English narration is followed by the Spanish narration.
Narration, Diana Munatones
Credits: Photography, Jean Berlfein.
Based on: The block book / Elizabeth S. Hirsch, editor.

 (Continued on next card)

A classroom with blocks [filmstrip] ... c1979.   (Card 2)

Sound accompaniment compatible for manual and automatic
operation.
    Summary: Shows ways preschool and early elementary children can
use blocks for both playing and learning. Describes skills children
learn by using blocks, such as building maps and models. Stresses the
value of play as a learning experience.

    1. Preschool education. 2. Elementary education. 3. Block
building (Education) 4. Play. I. Berlfein, Jean. II. Tyor, Terry.
III. National Association for the Education of Young Children.
IV. Title: The block book.

Example of a set of two filmstrips with sound cassettes, cataloged as a set. The second part-title varies slightly on filmstrip container (& instead of and).

037	‡a FFH 349 ‡b Films for the Humanities
245 04	‡a The nineteenth-century novel ‡h [filmstrip] / ‡c written by Carroll Moulton ; produced by Stephen Mantell.
246 3	‡a 19th century novel
260	‡a Princeton, N.J. : ‡b Films for the Humanities, Inc., ‡c c1981.
300	‡a 2 filmstrips (179 fr.) : ‡b col. and b&w ; ‡c 35 mm. + ‡e 2 sound cassettes (29 min.) + 1 teacher's guide ([7] p. ; 22 cm.).
440 0	‡a English literature, a survey ; ‡v unit 11
500	‡a Title on sound cassettes: The 19th century novel.
500	‡a Title on container for first filmstrip: Austen, the Brontës, & George Eliot.
508	‡a Editor, Carroll Moulton.
500	‡a Sound accompaniment compatible for manual and automatic operation.
504	‡a Guide includes background information about the novelists, study questions, and bibliographical references.
520	‡a Highlights English literature of the nineteenth century by focusing on the novels of Jane Austen, Charlotte and Emily Brontë, George Eliot, Charles Dickens, and William Thackeray.
505 0	‡a filmstrip 1. Austen, the Brontës, and George Eliot (92 fr., 15 min.) -- filmstrip 2. Dickens and Thackeray (87 fr., 14 min.).
650 8	‡a English fiction ‡x History and criticism.
600 18	‡a Austen, Jane, ‡d 1775-1817.
600 18	‡a Brontë, Charlotte, ‡d 1816-1855.
600 18	‡a Brontë, Emily, ‡d 1818-1848.
600 18	‡a Eliot, George, ‡d 1812-1870.
600 18	‡a Thackeray, William Makepeace, ‡d 1811-1863.
700 1	‡a Moulton, Carroll.
700 1	‡a Mantell, Stephen.
710 2	‡a Films for the Humanities (Firm)
740 02	‡a Austen, the Brontës, and George Eliot.
740 02	‡a Austen, the Brontës, & George Eliot.
740 02	‡a Dickens and Thackeray.

Example of a two-part sound slide set. There is no 300 ‡c because the slides are the standard size.

245 00	‡a Hatshepsut ‡h [slide] : ‡b the first woman of history / ‡c written by Doris Knotts.
246 30	‡a First woman of history
260	‡a Stanford, Calif. : ‡b Multi-Media Productions, Inc., ‡c c1975.
300	‡a 122 slides : ‡b col. + ‡e 1 sound cassette (26 min.) + 1 guide (8 p. ; 22 cm.).
500	‡a Sound accompaniment compatible for manual and automatic operation.
520	‡a Tells the story of Hatshepsut, the only daughter of Thutmose I's royal wife, who lived in ancient Egypt and eventually became Pharaoh. Discusses her contributions both as a royal leader and as a woman.
505 0	‡a pt. 1 (64 slides, 13 min.) -- pt. 2 (58 slides, 13 min.).
600 08	‡a Hatshepsut, ‡c Queen of Egypt.
651 8	‡a Egypt ‡x Kings and rulers.
651 8	‡a Egypt ‡x History.
700 1	‡a Knotts, Doris.
710 2	‡a Multi-Media Productions.

Example of a slide set with no sound track. Accompanied by a guide with slide descriptions, and other printed materials. There is no date on slides. Date is an inferred publication date based on copyright of guide. Slides do not have numbers. Numbers could be added on the slide mounts with a small-tipped marker, in case the slides are dropped, and omit the third 5XX note saying the slides are unnumbered. If important to the local library, artists listed in the 520 Summary Note can be traced in 600 subject fields. However, they can be found through keyword search if 600 subject headings are not added.

245 04	‡a The inquiring eye. ‡p American paintings ‡h [slide].	
246 30	‡a American paintings	
260	‡a Washington, D.C. : ‡b National Gallery of Art, ‡c [1992]	
300	‡a 20 slides : ‡b col. + ‡e 1 guide (48 p. : ill. 31 cm.) + 12 prints (col. ; 28 x 36 cm.) + 1 timeline poster (col. ; 61 x 91 cm.).	
500	‡a Title from guide.	
508	‡a Text, William Kloss.	
500	‡a Slides are labeled but unnumbered.	
500	‡a Guide includes background information and slide descriptions.	
520	‡a Introduces the development of painting in America from the mid-17th to the early 20th century and discusses the historical and cultural content within this period. Artists include John Singleton Copley, Gilbert Stuart, Rembrandt Peale, James Peale, Joshua Johnson, Edward Hicks, Thomas Cole, Albert Pinkham Ryder, Winslow Homer, Thomas Eakins, James McNeill Whistler, William Merritt Chase, Henry Ossawa Tanner, and George Bellows.	
650 8	‡a American painting ‡x History.	
700 1	‡a Kloss, William.	
710 2	‡a National Gallery of Art (U.S.)	

CHAPTER 5
CATALOGING NONPROJECTED GRAPHICS

Nonprojected graphics include pictures, posters, study prints, flannel board sets, activity cards, flash cards, art works, flip charts, technical drawings, etc. Rules are found in AACR2R Chapter 8, the same chapter as for filmstrips and slides. Transparencies are also found in Chapter 8.

Carefully examine the contents of boxes containing these items. Make sure all components are there. There is usually a guide that tells what components are in the set and how they are used. If there is no guide, look in the distributor's catalog for this information. If any component is missing, contact the distributor.

Chief Source of Information

The item itself (i.e., picture, poster, flannel board piece, activity card, etc.) is the Chief Source of Information. Usually these items will have a title printed on them. If not, the substitute Chief Source of Information can be (in this order): the container; accompanying textual material such as a guide; or other sources, such as the distributor's catalog.

GMD (245 ‡h)

This varies according to the type of item. Refer to AACR2R Chapter 1 for a list of official GMDs (also see Chapter 1 of this book, p. 6).

Physical Description Area (300 field)

The 300 field varies according to the format. Examples are in AACR2R. If only one kind of item is in the set (such as study prints, or pictures, or activity cards), list these items in the Extent of Item Area (300 ‡a). Other Physical Details (300 ‡b) will refer to the items in the Extent of Item Area (e.g., **b&w** or **col.**). Dimensions (300 ‡c) may be either the dimensions of the items themselves, or of the container in which they are stored if the items are not the same size. If the dimensions of the container are used, measure length x width x height of the box in centimeters, and precede these dimensions with the words **in container** (see example on p. 102).

For items using the GMD **[kit]**, in the Extent of Item Area (300 ‡a) list the components (see example, p. 102). Also list the components in 300 ‡a for kit-like materials in which one medium is predominant (see example, p. 95), or list the predominant medium in the Extent of Item Area and list the other components as accompanying materials. If there are too many types of items in a kit to list in the Extent of Item Area, use instead the phrase **various pieces** and use the Note Area to provide a more complete description of what is included (e.g., a 505 Contents Note).

Notes (5XX fields)

If the title is taken from a source other than the item itself (e.g., the container), make a 500 Source of Title Note. Titles may vary on the different components, guide, container, and in the distributor's catalog. List variant titles in a 500 note and trace them in a 246 field. Include a 520 Summary Note. Also include a 505 Contents Note if appropriate.

Subject Headings and Added Entries (6XX and 7XX fields)

In general, use subject headings as for a book or other item. Flannel board sets may also have the LC subject heading **Flannel boards** (650 field). Sears does not have a subject heading for flannel board sets. Added entries are as for other nonbook materials.

Examples follow.

Example of a flannel board set. Sears does not have a subject heading for flannel board sets, so the Library of Congress subject heading Flannel boards **is used below.**

037	‡a 88-1 ‡b Judy/Instructo
245 00	‡a Farm animals and babies ‡h [picture].
250	‡a Rev. ed.
260	‡a Minneapolis, MN : ‡b Judy/Instructo ; ‡a [Grandview, Mo. : ‡b Distributed by Constructive Playthings, ‡c 198-?]
300	‡a 21 pictures, 21 word cards, 1 teaching guide (2 p. ; 28 cm.) : ‡b col. ; ‡c in container, 31 x 47 x 3 cm.
500	‡a Title from container.
521 8	‡a For primary students.
520	‡a Flannel board set that contains pictures of common farm animals and their babies, along with word cards for each. Includes pictures of a hen, chicks, rooster, eggs, cow, bull, calf, steer, mare, colt, work horse, goat, kid, ewe, lamb, sow, piglets, duck, ducklings, goose, and turkey.
650 8	‡a Animal babies.
650 8	‡a Domestic animals.
650 8	‡a Livestock.
650 0	‡a Flannel boards.
710 2	‡a Judy/Instructo (Firm)
710 2	‡a Constructive Playthings.

Example of a set of activity cards with variant titles. This GMD was added to the list of official GMDs in AACR2R a few years ago. The Library of Congress does not use this GMD at present, but other libraries do use it.

020 ‡a 0886793513

037 ‡a 9104 ‡b Educational Insights

245 04 ‡a The art box ‡h [activity card] : ‡b for primary grades.

246 3 ‡a Art box : ‡b 150 creative art activities for primary grade studies

246 3 ‡a 150 creative art activities for primary grade studies

246 3 ‡a One hundred fifty creative art activities for primary grade studies

246 3 ‡a Art box, primary

260 ‡a Compton, CA : ‡b Educational Insights ; ‡a [Grandview, Mo. : ‡b Distributed by Constructive Playthings], ‡c c1971.

300 ‡a 153 activity cards : ‡b b&w ; ‡c in container, 11 x 17 x 8 cm. + ‡e 15 dividers.

500 ‡a Title on container: The art box : 150 creative art activities for primary grade studies.

500 ‡a Title in distributor's catalog: The art box--primary.

521 8 ‡a For grades K-3.

520 ‡a Includes 150 art activities, each complete with method, materials, and illustrations. Activity categories are: back to school; holiday crafts; clay; paper crafts; printing; drawing; painting; string, yarn and rope; puppets; wood crafts; sculpture; scrap crafts; murals; paper boxes; and decorations.

650 8 ‡a Art ‡x Study and teaching.

650 8 ‡a Handicraft.

710 2 ‡a Educational Insights (Firm)

710 2 ‡a Constructive Playthings.

Catalog card version:

The art box [activity card] : for primary grades.– Compton, Calif. :
    Educational Insights ; [Grandview, Mo. : Distributed by
    Constructive Playthings], c1971.
      153 activity cards : b&w ; in container, 11 x 17 x 8 cm. + 15
    dividers.

    Title on container: The art box : 150 creative art activities for
primary grade studies.
    Title in distributor's catalog: The art box--primary.
    For grades K-3.
    Summary: Includes 150 art activities, each complete with method,
materials, and illustrations. Activity categories are: back to school;

 (Continued on next card)

The art box [activity card] ... c1971.   (Card 2)

holiday crafts; clay; paper crafts; printing; drawing; painting; string;
yarn and rope; puppets; wood crafts; sculpture; scrap crafts; murals;
paper boxes; and decorations.
    ISBN 0-88679-351-3

    1. Art--Study and teaching. 2. Handicraft. I. Educational Insights
(Firm) II. Constructive Playthings. III. Title: Art box : 150 creative art
activities for primary grade studies. IV. Title: 150 creative art
activities for primary grade studies. V. Title: Art box, primary.

Example of a poster. Contains a collection of political cartoons. Names of artists of cartoons in 505 Contents Note were incomplete on item, and not all of the artists could be identified.

245 02 ‡a An age of reform, 1892-1919 ‡h [picture].

260 ‡a Fort Atkinson, WI : ‡b Highsmith Inc. ; ‡a [Culver City, Calif. : ‡b Distributed by Social Studies School Service], ‡c c1995.

300 ‡a 1 poster : ‡b ill. ; ‡c 61 x 96 cm. + ‡e 1 teacher's guide (7 p. : ill. ; 28 cm.).

440 0 ‡a U.S. history through cartoons

440 0 ‡a MindSparks

500 ‡a Title from teacher's guide.

500 ‡a "MindSparks, interactive learning tool from Highsmith"--guide cover.

520 ‡a Part of a series of posters showing political cartoons intended to help students appreciate the spirit of the times and the central concerns of these reform years from the point of view of people who lived during them. This poster shows six cartoons highlighting major themes of a time of rapid industrial growth and political reform. A growing concentration of power in the hands of giant industrial corporations accompanied America's transition in these years from a nation of small towns and local organizations to one of huge, diverse cities and impersonal institutions. In the late 1800s, a variety of reform movements responded to these changes, and to the problems they caused for farmers, workers, immigrant groups, small entrepreneurs and others. This reform era came at a time when America was also flexing its muscles on the world stage in a new way. Together, these trends made this a time of ferment and national assertiveness. Cartoons feature Presidents Theodore Roosevelt and Woodrow Wilson.

505 0 ‡a Bosses of the Senate / J. Keppler -- A party of patches / Gillam -- Good trusts, bad trusts / Berryman -- The world's constable / Aelrymple -- The python / J.N. "Ding" Darling -- The perfect soldier / Robert Minor.

651 8 ‡a United States ‡x Politics and government ‡y 1865-1898 ‡v Cartoons and caricatures.

651 8 ‡a United States ‡x Politics and government ‡y 1898-1919 ‡v Cartoons and caricatures.

600 18 ‡a Roosevelt, Theodore, ‡d 1858-1919 ‡v Cartoons and caricatures.

600 18 ‡a Wilson, Woodrow, ‡d 1856-1924 ‡v Cartoons and caricatures.

700 1 ‡a Keppler, Udo J., ‡d 1872-1956.

700 1 ‡a Darling, Jay N. ‡q (Jay Norwood), ‡d 1876-1962.

700 1 ‡a Minor, Robert, ‡d 1884-1952.

710 2 ‡a Highsmith Inc.

710 2 ‡a Social Studies School Service.

Catalog card version:

An age of reform, 1892-1919 [picture]. -- Fort Atkinson, WI :
    Highsmith Inc. ; [Culver City, Calif. : Distributed by Social Studies
    School Service], c1995.
        1 poster : ill. ; 61 x 96 cm. + 1 teacher's guide (7 p. : ill. ; 28
    cm.). -- (U.S. history through cartoons) (MindSparks)

Title from teacher's guide.
"MindSparks, interactive learning tool from Highsmith"--guide
cover.
    Summary: Part of a series showing political cartoons intended to
help students appreciate the spirit of the times and the central concerns
of these reform years from the point of view of people who lived
during them. This poster shows six cartoons highlighting major themes
of a time of rapid industrial growth and political reform. A growing

 (Continued on next card)

An age of reform, 1892-1919 [picture] ... c1995.   (Card 2)

concentration of power in the hands of giant industrial corporations
accompanied America's transition in these years from a nation of small
towns and local organizations to one of huge, diverse cities and
impersonal institutions. In the late 1800s, a variety of reform
movements responded to these changes, and to the problems they
caused for farmers, workers, immigrant groups, small entrepreneurs
and others. This reform era came at a time when America was also
flexing its muscles on the world stage in a new way. Together, these
trends made this a time of ferment and national assertiveness. Cartoons
feature Presidents Theodore Roosevelt and Woodrow Wilson.

 (Continued on next card)

An age of reform, 1892-1919 [picture] ... c1995.   (Card 3)

    Contents: Bosses of the Senate / J. Keppler -- A party of patches /
Gillam -- Good trusts, bad trusts / Berryman -- The world's constable /
Aelrymple -- The python / J.N. "Ding" Darling -- The perfect soldier /
Robert Minor.
    1. United States--Politics and government--1865-1898--Cartoons
and caricatures. 2. United States--Politics and government--1898-
1919--Cartoons and caricatures. 3. Roosevelt, Theodore, 1858-1919--
Cartoons and caricatures. 4. Wilson, Woodrow, 1856-1924--Cartoons
and caricatures. I. Keppler, Udo J., 1872-1956. II. Darling, Jay N.
(Jay Norwood), 1876-1962. III. Minor, Robert, 1884-1952.
IV. Highsmith Inc. V. Social Studies School Service.

Example of a set of flash cards for children. Currently the Library of Congress does not use this GMD, but other libraries do.

037	‡a 1104 ‡b Kenworthy Educational Service, Inc.
245 00	‡a Phonic picture cards ‡h [flash card].
260	‡a Buffalo, N.Y. : ‡b Kenworthy Educational Service, Inc. ; ‡a [Grandview, Mo. : ‡b Distributed by Constructive Playthings], ‡c c1976.
300	‡a 55 picture cards : ‡b col. ; ‡c 14 x 18 cm. + ‡e 1 instruction card.
500	‡a Title from container.
521 8	‡a For grades 1-3.
520	‡a Includes all the phonic sounds introduced in beginning reading, plus more advanced blends used in second and third grades. Teaches initial consonants, long and short vowel sounds, y as long i and e, r syllables, diphthongs and digraphs, beginning and ending double consonants, and initial and final triple consonants. Can be used as a tool for drill, remediation and group or individual reinforcement.
650 8	‡a Reading ‡x Phonetic method.
650 8	‡a English language ‡x Pronunciation.
650 8	‡a Phonetics.
710 2	‡a Kenworthy Educational Service.
710 2	‡a Constructive Playthings.

Example of a set of flash cards for teens and adults.

245 04 ‡a The I can ‡h [flash card] : ‡b 101 cards of personal affirmation.

246 30 ‡a 101 cards of personal affirmation

246 3 ‡a One hundred one cards of personal affirmation

260 ‡a Bellevue, Wash. : ‡b G.B.E. Publishers, Inc., ‡c [1996]

300 ‡a 101 flash cards : ‡b b&w ; ‡c 9 x 11 cm. + ‡e 1 information sheet.

500 ‡a Title from container.

508 ‡a Original card set, Richard M. Eberle, Margaret Gerharz, Gerald Bongard ; information sheet, Richard M. Eberle.

500 ‡a Date and publisher on container and cards, c1985, G²BE Publishers, Inc. Date and publisher on information sheet, c1996, G.B.E. Publishers, Inc.

500 ‡a In a round can container, 12 cm. high.

520 ‡a Set of flash cards teaches positive thinking and self-actualization. Teaches life skills to accentuate the positive and eliminate the negative, to replace old negative scripts with new self-affirming scripts. Focuses on the concept that "whether you think you can or you think you can't, you're right." Each card has one affirmation in bold print and an introduction to that statement. Can be used in groups or in individual sessions for increasing self-esteem and self-worth.

650 8 ‡a Self-esteem.

650 8 ‡a Conduct of life.

650 8 ‡a Success.

700 1 ‡a Eberle, Richard M.

700 1 ‡a Gerharz, Margaret.

700 1 ‡a Bongard, Gerald.

710 2 ‡a G.B.E. Publishers.

Example of a kit (set of printed material that must be kept together). Subject heading is borrowed from the Library of Congress since Sears does not have an appropriate subject heading.

100 1	‡a Hill, Herbert D.	
245 14	‡a The outlining kit ‡h [kit] / ‡c by Herbert D. Hill, Jr. and M. Joan McKenna.	
260	‡a North Billerica, Mass. : ‡b Curriculum Associates, Inc., ‡c c1977.	
300	‡a 115 lesson and review cards, 7 dividers, 9 spirit masters, 1 teacher's guide ; ‡c in container, 17 x 24 x 9 cm.	
521 8	‡a Designed for grades 5-9.	
520	‡a Provides activities to help students develop basic skills in outlining.	
505 0	‡a Finding main topics (Lessons 1-10) -- Classifying parts of outlines (Lessons 11-50) -- Developing complete outlines (Lessons 51-70) -- Using details (Lessons 71-84) -- Writing complete outlines (Lessons 85-94) -- Writing paragraphs from outlines (Lessons 95-99).	
650 0	‡a Outlines.	
650 8	‡a English language ‡x Composition and exercises.	
700 1	‡a McKenna, M. Joan.	
710 2	‡a Curriculum Associates, Inc.	

Example of a kit (collection of printed material that must be kept together). Main entry is under personal name. Title must be traced under acronym with and without periods.

020   ‡a 0942097491 (student workbook)

020   ‡a 0942097475 (facilitator's guide)

020   ‡a 0942097300 (journal)

100 2   ‡a Roth-Nelson, Stephanie, ‡d 1949-

245 10   ‡a S.E.E.K. ‡h [kit] : ‡b self-esteem enhancement kit / ‡c Stephanie Roth-Nelson.

246 30   ‡a Self-esteem enhancement kit

246 3   ‡a SEEK, self-esteem enhancement kit

246 3   ‡a S.E.E.K. program

246 3   ‡a SEEK program

260   ‡a Louisville, Colo. : ‡b Center for Adolescent Self-Esteem : ‡b BBPbooks, ‡c c1997.

300   ‡a 1 student workbook (168 p. : ill. ; 18 x 22 cm.), 1 facilitator's guide (134 p. ; 28 cm.), 1 journal (unpaged ; 27 cm.), 45 blackline masters (28 cm.).

500   ‡a Title on worksheet masters: The S.E.E.K. program.

500   ‡a Joint author for facilitator's guide, Nancy Jessop Conway.

520   ‡a Provides activities to help teenagers improve self-esteem and cope with life, adults, school, and each other. Encourages trust in adults as positive role models. Activities center on feelings/emotions, cognitive/thinking, and life skills/practical.

505 0   ‡a Trust -- I never had a childhood -- Problem solving using dialogues -- Happiness -- Religion vs. spirituality -- Choices -- I hate school (I'm not dumb) -- Are you different? -- Beliefs and values -- Anger -- Art is -- Taking risks -- How to deal with abusive people (School settings ; Detention/treatment settings) -- My personal rights -- No one listens to me -- Novel concepts -- Depression -- Blame (If only--) -- Drugs, drinking, sex -- I'm bored -- Who's that talking? -- Grief and loss -- Unhealthy eating habits -- I'm tired of being a latch-key kid -- Appreciating yourself -- Goal setting (I wish I was more--) -- I hate holidays -- Get a job! -- Finding a guiding light.

650 8 ‡a Self-esteem.

650 8 ‡a Adolescent psychology.

650 8 ‡a Teenagers.

700 1 ‡a Conway, Nancy Jessop.

710 2 ‡a Center for Adolescent Self-Esteem.

710 2 ‡a BBPbooks (Firm)

Example of a poster with variant titles. Series is in 830 because it comes from the distributor's catalog.

037	‡a 1337 ‡b Pomegranate Publications
245 00	‡a Langston Hughes (1902-1967) ‡h [picture] : ‡b poet laureate of Harlem.
246 30	‡a Poet laureate of Harlem
246 3	‡a Langston Hughes (American, 1902-1967)
246 3	‡a Langston Hughes poster
260	‡a Rohnert Park, CA : ‡b Pomegranate Publications in association with What's a Face Productions ; ‡a Culver City, CA : ‡b Social Studies School Service [distributor], ‡c [1993?]
300	‡a 1 poster : ‡b sepia ; ‡c 92 x 61 cm.
500	‡a Title in credits information at bottom of poster: Langston Hughes (American, 1902-1967).
500	‡a Title on container: Langston Hughes poster.
508	‡a Designed by Tim Lewis.
500	‡a Series in distributor's catalog: Black history poster series.
520	‡a Sepia photograph of Afro-American poet Langston Hughes.
600 18	‡a Hughes, Langston, ‡d 1902-1967.
650 8	‡a African Americans ‡x History.
700 1	‡a Lewis, Tim.
710 2	‡a Pomegranate Publications.
710 2	‡a What's a Face Productions.
710 2	‡a Social Studies School Service.
830 0	‡a Black history poster series.

CHAPTER 6
CATALOGING THREE-DIMENSIONAL MATERIALS

These items include models, dioramas, games, toys, puzzles, sculptures, and realia (naturally occurring objects). Rules are found in AACR2R Chapter 10.

Carefully examine the contents of boxes containing these items. Make sure all components are there. There is usually a guide that tells how many components are in the set and how they are used. If there is no guide, look in the distributor's catalog for this information. If any component is missing, contact the distributor.

Chief Source of Information

The Chief Source of Information is the item itself, together with accompanying textual material and container. Prefer information on the item itself if there is a conflict.

GMD (245 ‡h)

Schools most frequently catalog games, puzzles, and models. Some may catalog puppets and other toys. The GMD (245 ‡h) for both games and puzzles is [game]. For models, the GMD is [model]. For puppets and other toys, the GMD is [toy]. If actual items (rocks, etc.) are cataloged in the library collection, use the GMD [realia]. Other GMDs are found in AACR2R, Chapter 1.

Physical Description Area (300 field)

The Extent of Item (300 ‡a) for games will be similar to nonprojected graphics that use the GMD [kit]: list the components. The Extent of Item for puzzles will be the number of pieces in the puzzle (if describing only one puzzle) or the number of puzzles if cataloging a set. Other Physical Details (300 ‡b) should state what material was used in making the item, with information on color: if one color or two colors, the colors are named; if more than two colors, use **col.**; or use **b&w** if applicable. Dimensions (300 ‡c) for games and puzzles will be either the size of the puzzle when it is put together, or **in container** with the container's dimensions.

Notes (5XX fields)

Notes are very important. Title variations should appear in a 500 note and should be traced. Additional information about physical characteristics might be needed. Usually a 520 Summary Note is needed, so that the user can tell how the item is used and for whom it might be intended. Add a 505 Contents Note if appropriate.

Subject Headings and Added Entries (6XX and 7XX fields)

Assign subject headings as for other formats. For games, catalogers may assign the 650 subject heading **Educational games** or **Games** (if not really educational). For puzzles, use subject heading **Puzzles**. Added entries are as for other AV formats.

Examples follow.

Example of a game. Title needs several 246 fields for computer access.

037	‡a LKE 1402 ‡b Little Kenny Publications
245 00	‡a Little Kenny's flip 'n skip ‡h [game] : ‡b outdoor-indoor play 'n learn game for children 4 to 10.
246 30	‡a Flip 'n skip
246 30	‡a Outdoor-indoor play 'n learn game for children 4 to 10
246 3	‡a Outdoor-indoor play and learn game for children 4 to 10
246 3	‡a Little Kenny's flip and skip
246 3	‡a Flip and skip
260	‡a Chicago, Ill. : ‡b Little Kenny Publications ; ‡a [Grandview, Mo. : ‡b Distributed by Constructive Playthings], ‡c c1971.
300	‡a 1 vinyl playfield, 1 spinner, 2 bean bags, 1 instruction sheet : ‡b col. ; ‡c in container, 46 x 31 x 4 cm.
521 8	‡a For ages 4-10.
520	‡a Includes three games designed to help students learn math skills through physical exercise. Play is based on use of a vinyl mat showing numbers 1-12, on which players step or throw a bean bag.
650 8	‡a Arithmetic ‡x Study and teaching.
650 8	‡a Educational games.
650 8	‡a Mathematical recreations.
710 2	‡a Little Kenny Publications.
710 2	‡a Constructive Playthings.

Catalog card version:

Little Kenny's flip 'n skip [game] : outdoor-indoor play 'n learn game
    for children 4 to 10. -- Chicago, Ill. : Little Kenny Publications ;
    [Grandview, Mo. : Distributed by Constructive Playthings], c1971.
       1 vinyl playfield, 1 spinner, 2 bean bags, 1 instruction sheet :
    col. ; in container, 46 x 31 x 4 cm.

For ages 4-10.
Summary: Includes three games designed to help students learn
math skills through physical exercise. Play is based on use of a vinyl
mat showing numbers 1-12, on which players step or throw a bean bag.

 (Continued on next card)

Little Kenny's flip 'n skip [game] ... c1971.   (Card 2)

    1. Arithmetic--Study and teaching. 2. Educational games.
3. Mathematical recreations. I. Little Kenny Publications. II.
Constructive Playthings. III. Title: Flip 'n skip. IV. Title: Outdoor-
indoor play 'n learn game for children 4 to 10. V. Title: Outdoor-
indoor play and learn game for children 4 to 10. VI. Title: Little
Kenny's flip and skip. VII. Flip and skip.

Example of a children's game.

037	‡a 360 ‡b Cadaco
245 04	‡a The Goldilocks and the three bears game ‡h [game].
246 3	‡a Goldilocks and three bears
260	‡a Chicago, Ill. : ‡b Cadaco, Inc. ; ‡a [Grandview, Mo. : ‡b Distributed by Constructive Playthings], ‡c c1973.
300	‡a 1 game board, 7 cards, 4 pawns, 1 spinner card : ‡b cardboard and plastic, col. ; ‡c in container, 25 x 49 x 4 cm.
440 0	‡a Cadaco storybook classic game
500	‡a Title in distributor's catalog: Goldilocks and three bears.
500	‡a Instructions on bottom of box.
521 8	‡a For ages 3-8.
520	‡a Game based on the fairy tale. Involves color and/or object matching and following directions with no reading involved. For 2 to 4 players.
650 8	‡a Games.
650 8	‡a Fairy tales.
710 2	‡a Cadaco, Inc.
710 2	‡a Constructive Playthings.

Example of a game for teenagers and adults.

245 00   ‡a Together ‡h [game].

250   ‡a Rev.

260   ‡a Beachwood, OH : ‡b Wellness Reproductions & Pub. Inc., ‡c c1990.

300   ‡a 35 cards, 1 instruction sheet : ‡b b&w ; ‡c in container, 3 x 10 x 7 cm.

500   ‡a Publishing information from sticker covering original imprint: Creative Games, Wyoming, Mich.

521 8   ‡a For teenagers and adults.

520   ‡a Game in which players work together in pairs to accomplish unique tasks on game cards physically, non-verbally and verbally. Partners will exercise cooperation and teamwork as they learn more about each other. Cards suggest creative action experiences that are challenging and enjoyable.

650   8   ‡a Games.

710 2   ‡a Wellness Reproductions & Publishing Inc.

710 2   ‡a Creative Games (Firm)

Example of a puzzle. There is no GMD [puzzle]. The closest GMD is [game].

037	‡a 165 ‡b Incentives for Learning
245 00	‡a Long and short vowel puzzles ‡h [game].
260	‡a Chicago, Ill. : ‡b Incentives for Learning, Inc., ‡c c1979.
300	‡a 20 reversible puzzles (4 pieces each) : ‡b col. ; ‡c 21 x 10 cm. + ‡e 1 guide (3 p. ; 22 cm.).
520	‡a Half of the puzzles match sounds to pictures; half of the puzzles match sounds to words. Designed for the elementary non-reader as well as the student who can identify written words.
650 8	‡a English language ‡x Study and teaching.
650 8	‡a English language ‡x Pronunciation.
650 8	‡a Phonetics.
650 8	‡a Puzzles.
710 2	‡a Incentives for Learning, Inc.

Example of a hand puppet. The series and producer's name and address were on the same cloth tag with washing instructions. Some puppets also have a cardboard hang-tag with the name of the puppet. Sometimes there is even a copyright date on one of the tags. But this puppet was missing its hang-tag and the other tag did not have a date. The cataloger supplied a title.

245 00	‡a [Lobster hand puppet] ‡h [toy].
246 3	‡a Lobster puppet
260	‡a Emeryville, CA : ‡b Folkmanis, Inc., ‡c [199-?]
300	‡a 1 hand puppet : ‡b fabric, red ; ‡c 62 x 26 x 9 cm.
440 0	‡a Folktails
500	‡a Title supplied by cataloger.
500	‡a Made of 100% polyester; surface washable; air dry.
520	‡a Right-handed glove puppet, red lobster with black eyes. For large hand. Moves front claws and three legs on right side.
650 8	‡a Puppets and puppet plays.
710 2	‡a Folkmanis, Inc.

Example of a model.

037	‡a J209040 ‡b Judy/Instructo
245 00	‡a Original Judy clock ‡h [model].
246 30	‡a Judy clock
260	‡a Minneapolis : ‡b Judy/Instructo ; ‡a [Grandview, Mo. : ‡b Distributed by Constructive Playthings, ‡c 1984], c1975.
300	‡a 1 clock face : ‡b hardboard, col. ; ‡c 34 x 33 cm. + ‡e 2 metal stands + 1 guide (3 p. ; 28 cm.).
500	‡a Title in distributor's catalog: Judy clock.
521 8	‡a For ages 4 and up.
520	‡a Provides the face of a clock with movable plastic hands, visible working gears, numerals on face, and marks for minute and hour. With detachable legs. Can be used with: Original mini-clocks.
650 8	‡a Time.
650 8	‡a Clocks and watches.
710 2	‡a Judy/Instructo (Firm)
710 2	‡a Constructive Playthings.
740 0	‡a Original mini-clocks.

CHAPTER 7
CATALOGING SOUND RECORDINGS

AACR2R Rules for Cataloging Sound Formats

Use general rules for cataloging AV materials, including those in AACR2R Chapter 1, and rules in AACR2R Chapter 6 that are specifically for sound recordings. Chapter 6 applies to all sound formats, both musical and spoken recordings.

Format Dilemmas

New enhanced compact disc formats primarily used as computer software, but containing a portion that can be played in sound CD players, are cataloged as computer formats. If a sound CD includes only a track or two for computer, catalog it as a sound recording with a note about the computer track, and include a 538 System Requirements Note.

A book with identical sound cassette may be cataloged either as a book with accompanying sound cassette or a sound cassette with accompanying book, depending on whether the main purpose is for the user to read the book or to hear the sound cassette. A read-along set with book and sound cassette should be cataloged as a sound cassette (see example on p. 133). For some book and cassette combinations, a case can be made to catalog them as kits, if in the cataloger's judgment neither format predominates. In practice, catalogers may choose any of the three ways to catalog a book/cassette pair.

Previewing

Many AV catalogers do not preview sound recordings due to the time involved. Running times are often on these items or in the accompanying printed material.

If a cataloger decides not to preview sound cassettes, it is important to make sure that the recorded program matches the label and that the cassette will advance and rewind. If sound cassettes and records are previewed, note the running time of each side for possible use in a 505 Contents Note. If there are two or more spoken segments or musical works on each side, and it is important to users to know the running times of each individual part, put the individual running times in the 505 Contents Note. Put the total running time of the sound recording (all cassettes or discs in the set) in the Extent of Item area (300 ‡a).

Multi-Part Sound Recordings

If a nonmusical record or cassette contains a separate, self-contained work on each side, unrelated to what is on the reverse side, catalog each side as a separate program. A similar music recording with no collective title is usually cataloged as one unit (see example below under GMD). If a multi-part sound recording (i.e., two or more cassettes, records, or CDs) comes in a container with a collective title, use the collective title as the Title Proper and put the titles of the separate works in a 505 Contents Note.

Chief Source of Information

For sound cassettes and records, the Chief Source of Information is the label attached to the item (all sides). For a compact disc, the Chief Source of Information is the item itself, where information is usually printed directly on the disc. The disc surface is still called a label in 5XX notes. For a set, look for a collective title. If the individual labels do not furnish a collective title, use the collective title from another source as the Title Proper. Choose a substitute Chief Source of Information from the following sources (in this order): accompanying textual material (guide, script, libretto, etc.); container; or other sources, such as the distributor's catalog. For CDs and sound cassettes, information visible through a closed container (e.g., on front cover of booklet inserted in container lid, appearing as container cover) is considered to be "on container" for purposes of source notes.

Title Proper (245 ‡a)

The title in the 245 field is the title on the Chief Source of Information. If spoken data (e.g., spoken title) conflicts with printed data, prefer the printed data. Make a note giving the spoken title and trace it in a 246 field. If the title of the recording is only the name of the performing group, use that as the 245 title, and do not put the performing group in the Statement of Responsibility (see example on p. 122).

GMD (245 ‡h)

For sound cassettes, records, or compact discs, the GMD is **[sound recording]**, placed after the Title Proper. For music sound recordings of two or more separate works that have no collective title, the separate works appear in 245 with the first title in ‡a, followed by the GMD in 245 ‡h, and subsequent titles in ‡b. Examples:

> Several works with the same Statement of Responsibility:
> **245 13** ‡a La mer ‡h **[GMD]** ; ‡b Khamma ; Rhapsody for clarinet and orchestra / ‡c Claude Debussy.
> (Main entry will be the composer. Individual works will be traced in ‡t of 700 fields under composer with indicators **12** since they represent contents.)

> Several works with different Statements of Responsibility:
> **245 10** ‡a Prelude, the afternoon of a faun ‡h **[GMD]** / ‡c Claude Debussy. Peer Gynt (Suite) no. 1-2 / Edvard Grieg. Till Eulenspiegels lustige Streiche / Richard Strauss.
> (Main entry will be the first named composer. Other composers will be traced in 700 12 with ‡t for their work.)

Statement of Responsibility (245 ‡c)

Usually the Statement of Responsibility (245 ‡c) will include the "responsible" persons or corporate bodies that appear prominently along with the title on the Chief Source of Information. For music, this is likely to be the composer and/or major performers or performing groups. Some AV catalogers prefer to put performers and performing groups in a 511 Performer Note instead. For readings of literature, both author and reader may appear along with the title on the Chief Source of Information. If so, both may be put in the Statement of Responsibility (see example, p. 134). If the reader is named outside the Chief Source of Information, put the reader in a 511 Performer Note. For speeches, debates, and interviews, the speakers may appear along with the title on the Chief Source of Information and may be put in 245 ‡c.

Usually do not supply a bracketed Statement of Responsibility if none appears on the Chief Source of Information. Such information found elsewhere should appear in a note. At times, however, bracketed words should be inserted into the Statement of Responsibility to clarify the function of someone whose name appears on the Chief Source of Information. A name used by itself in the Statement of Responsibility implies intellectual responsibility for the contents. Occasionally a person is actually just a performer or reader but his name appears alone on the Chief Source of Information and his function is explained elsewhere. Insert a statement of function such as **[performed by]** or **[read by]** to show that the person is not the composer or author.

The producer of a sound recording is transcribed either in the Statement of Responsibility or in the 508 Credits Note. This is a recent change in cataloging practice. Previously, catalogers tended to omit the producer of a sound recording. The producer of a sound recording does not have the same degree of overall responsibility as the producer of a video program.

Date (260 field)

Dates on sound recordings (especially music) can become complicated when the work is reissued in another format, such as a record later released as a cassette or compact disc. CDs as a physical format were first available in 1982. Sound cassettes as a physical format were first available in 1965. LP (long playing) records were first available in 1948. Earlier dates on these respective formats usually indicate that the sound recording was previously released in an earlier format.

On the sound recording itself, a phonogram date may appear instead of a copyright date, e.g., **p1976** rather than **c1976**. The p-date is the equivalent of a copyright date for recorded sound. The container may have a later copyright date (preceded by **c**, not **p**), but this is usually the copyright of the container design rather than the date of the recorded program. Catalogers usually infer the copyright date on the container as the publication date and use it in brackets in 260 ‡c along with the p-date, e.g. **[1990], p1976**. This frequently happens with music CDs that were released earlier as LP records or sound cassettes.

Occasionally musical works are published that were recorded at a live performance some years earlier. Give this recording information in a 518 note.

Physical Description Area (300 field)

The 300 ‡a, Extent of Item, contains the appropriate SMD from AACR2R (see Chapter 1, p. 6), preceded by the number of items and followed by the total duration in parentheses. If the duration is stated on the item in minutes and seconds, the latest AACR2R rules say to transcribe both minutes and seconds in 300 ‡a. For example, if a label or container states the duration as **29 minutes, 30 seconds** (or as **29:30**), the running time in 300 ‡a is **(29 min., 30 sec.)**. This is a fairly recent rule change. Previously, catalogers rounded the duration stated on the item to the next minute up, and some still do this. If a previewer times the sound recording, round to the next minute up for 300 ‡a.

Some sound recordings may list only individual running times for songs or spoken segments instead of a total running time. These individual running times may be printed on the label of the sound recording, on the container, or on a printed sheet or booklet inserted in the container. Individual durations for songs or segments may be used to arrive at a quick "guesstimate" by considering seconds over 30 as an additional minute and ignoring seconds under 30. Thus, 2:35 would be 3 min., but 2:25 would be 2 min., as the cataloger mentally runs up a quick total. This quick calculation usually results in a running time within a minute or two of the actual total. If the running time is calculated this way, precede it with **ca.** in the Physical Description Area (see example on p. 120). If there is time to add individual running times more accurately, total and round to the next minute up for 300 ‡a. Do not just make a guess about the duration of a sound recording. If no total running time can be found or calculated, omit the duration from 300 ‡a.

In 300 ‡b, Other Physical Details, **analog** and **digital** refer to the way in which the recordings were made. Traditional LP records and standard sound cassettes use **analog** in 300 ‡b. Compact discs use **digital** in 300 ‡b. Some sound recordings state that they are monaural or monophonic (**mono.**), or stereophonic (**stereo.**). Others do not. When the item states one or the other, use the appropriate abbreviation. If the item does not specify either one, do not guess. Omit this information from 300 ‡b.

For 300 ‡c, Dimensions, standard CDs are **4 ¾ in.** Standard LP records are **12 in.** Cassettes omit dimensions unless they are a nonstandard size, such as miniatures.

Examples of the Physical Description Area are given in AACR2R Chapter 6. Following are some examples of 300 fields for sound formats.

For a standard sound cassette:

> 300   ‡a 1 sound cassette (60 min.) : ‡b analog, mono. + ‡e 1 script (20 p. ; 21 cm.).

For an LP record:

> 300   ‡a 1 sound disc (40 min.) : ‡b analog, 33 1/3 rpm, stereo. ; ‡c 12 in. + ‡e 1 booklet of program notes (16 p. ; 21 cm.).

For a sound CD:

> 300   ‡a 1 sound disc (58 min.) : ‡b digital, stereo. ; ‡c 4 3/4 in. + ‡e 1 booklet (14 p. ; 12 cm.).

For a record with the two sides cataloged separately:

> 300   ‡a on 1 side of 1 sound disc (20 min.) : ‡b analog, 33 1/3 rpm, stereo. ; ‡c 12 in.

Notes (5XX fields)

For a sound CD, the first note should be a 538 Format Note: **Compact disc**. This note was previously tagged 500 and appeared later in the note sequence as a Physical Description Note. In practice, catalogers may use either placement and either tag.

Some catalogers regard the three-letter code on sound CDs as important and add this three-letter code to the 538 Format Note. This is not a widespread practice but would be a local decision if this information is important to patrons. Following are definitions of the codes:

> **DDD**   Digital tape recorder used during session recording (D), mixing and/or editing (D), and mastering (transcription) (D)
>
> **ADD**   Analog tape recorder used during session recording (A); digital tape recorder used during subsequent mixing and/or editing (D) and during mastering (transcription) (D).
>
> **AAD**   Analog tape recorder used during session recording (A) and subsequent mixing and/or editing (A); digital tape recorder used during mastering (transcription) (D)

For music such as symphonies, vocal or instrumental ensembles, etc., the cataloging record may have a 511 Performer Note which lists the name of the performing group, orchestra or choir and director/conductor, and possibly individual performers such as instrumentalists or singers in groups. For operas or musicals, put soloists and actors/actresses in a 511 Cast Note. Trace important persons, orchestras, performing groups, etc. If there are too many to trace, a keyword search will still locate them. For spoken recordings, use a 511 Cast Note (first indicator 1) for drama or a 511 Performer Note (first indicator 0) for speakers, narrators, and readers. Trace important performers.

For spoken recordings, include a 520 Summary Note. For collections of short musical works, a 520 Summary Note may not be needed since the 505 Contents Note may give sufficient information. Always include a 505 Contents Note if the recording consists of a reasonable number of short segments. Contents are usually found on the label of the sound recording, the container, or in accompanying printed material. The value of a 505 Contents Note is that individual segments can be found with keyword search. If there are too many segments to put in a 505 Contents Note, include the most important items in the 520 Summary Note and they will still be found in a keyword search. If running times are found on the item for the individual works listed in the 505 field, add these in parentheses as stated on the item (see example on p. 120). For music, individual titles in the 505 field may be followed by space-slash-space and composers and/or major performers before the running time of the individual work in parentheses (see examples, p. 120-122).

For a cassette or disc with a separately-cataloged program on each side, the last note will be:

> 501   ‡a With: **Title of work on reverse side**.

See example on p. 131.

Subject Headings (6XX fields)

For nonfiction spoken recordings, assign subject headings as for books and educational videos. Subject headings for music recordings may be for the type of music, such as Sears subject headings **Opera**, **Symphony**, **Musicals**, **Jazz music**, **Popular music**, **Folk songs**, etc. Readings of literature may or may not have a subject heading, depending on how the work would be cataloged in book form. For example, a recorded reading of a novel or short story might have a subject heading with the form subdivision ‡v **Fiction** if this is how the same item would be cataloged in book form. The type of fiction may also appear as a subject heading, such as **Science fiction, Adventure fiction, Historical fiction, Western stories, Love stories, Western stories, Mystery fiction**, etc. **Talking books** is used for books read verbatim. Collections of poetry or short stories might have the subject heading **Poetry** ‡v **Collections** or **Short stories**, etc. A dramatic work might have a subject heading subdivided by ‡v **Drama**, such as **United States ‡x History ‡y 1861-1865, Civil War ‡v Drama**.

Added Entries (7XX fields)

Trace responsible people and corporate bodies as for other AV formats. Some catalogers do not trace the publishing company (260 ‡b) for sound recordings; others do. Added entries may be needed for performers or performing groups, speakers, etc., especially if they are well known. Use judgment based on what is needed for the local library. In most online systems, keyword search will locate individual names.

Trace series titles (usually in a 440 field) and variant titles (246 field). Trace a part-title from the 505 Contents Note in a 740 field if the work is a significant part of the recording or it is important to users to find it through a title search. In most online systems, it is possible to locate one song, poem, etc. using keyword search if that title is in the 505 Contents Note or 520 Summary Note. Use the 730 field to trace segments from radio programs. The title of a radio program in the 730 field will be followed by the qualifier **(Radio program)**.

If important to local patrons and the cataloger has time, 740 fields can be added for each song, poem, etc. in the 505 Contents Note so users will find these individual titles in an ordinary title search. Or, a 700 field (indicators 12) can be added for each writer or composer, with the title of the work in 700 ‡t. If these 700 fields with a ‡t are added, an author search will show all of these titles on the public index screen for easy scanning. Most online systems will automatically access the title in 700 ‡t in an ordinary title search, eliminating the need for a 740 title added entry. If the local online catalog accesses 700 ‡t in title searches, do not use <u>both</u> a 700 with the title in ‡t <u>and</u> an identical 740, or that title will index twice. Whether to add 700 fields or 740 fields based on a 505 Contents Note is a local decision. A keyword search will find all of these writers, composers, and titles if they are in the 505 Contents Note.

Examples follow.

Example of a CD containing excerpts from Haydn symphonies, with 240 Uniform Title. Symphony numbers in 700 fields are examples of special numbers assigned to the works of prolific musicians. Such headings are found in the OCLC authority file.

028 02   ‡a 423098-2 ‡b Archiv Produktion

100 1   ‡a Haydn, Joseph, ‡d 1732-1809.

240 10   ‡a Symphonies. ‡k Selections

245 10   ‡a Symphonies ‡h [sound recording] / ‡c Joseph Haydn.

260   ‡a Hamburg [Germany] : ‡b Archiv Produktion, ‡c p1987.

300   ‡a 1 sound disc (65 min.) : ‡b digital, stereo. ; ‡c 4 ¾ in. + ‡e 1 booklet (12 p. ; 12 cm.).

538   ‡a Compact disc.

511 0   ‡a Performance by English Concert ; Trevor Pinnock, conductor.

518   ‡a Recorded in Henry Wood Hall, London, Sept. 1986.

500   ‡a Program notes in booklet inserted in container.

505 0   ‡a Symphony no. 6 in D major, Hob.I:6, Le matin: Adagio, allegro (4:32) ; Adagio, andante, adagio (8:54) ; Menuet & trio (4:03) ; Finale, allegro (3:23) -- Symphony no. 7 in C major, Hob.I:7, Le midi: Adagio, allegro (5:50) ; Recitativo, adagio (9:16) ; Menuetto & trio (3:49) ; Finale, allegro (2:54) -- Symphony no. 8 in G major, Hob.I:8, Le soir: Allegro molto (3:53) ; Andante (9:16) ; Menuetto & trio (5:04) ; La tempesta, presto (3:30).

650 8   ‡a Symphony.

700 1   ‡a Pinnock, Trevor.

700 12   ‡a Haydn, Joseph, ‡d 1732-1809. ‡t Symphonies, ‡n H. I, 6, ‡r D major.

700 12   ‡a Haydn, Joseph, ‡d 1732-1809. ‡t Symphonies, ‡n H. I, 7, ‡r C major.

700 12   ‡a Haydn, Joseph, ‡d 1732-1809. ‡t Symphonies, ‡n H. I, 8, ‡r G major.

710 2   ‡a Archiv Produktion.

710 2   ‡a English Concert (Musical group)

Example of a music CD by an individual performer. Originally an LP record. Main entry is under the performer. Composers of individual songs appear in statements of responsibility in the 505 Contents Note. Composers are traced below in 700 fields, but not all libraries would trace them since they can be found through keyword search. This is a local decision. Another local decision is whether to trace individual song titles. This can be done in 700 ‡t or 740 fields if desired. They can also be found through keyword search.

028 02	VMD-79332 ‡b Vanguard
100 1	‡a Baez, Joan.
245 10	‡a Hits/greatest and others ‡h [sound recording] / ‡c Joan Baez.
246 3	‡a Greatest hits
260	‡a Santa Monica, CA : ‡b Vanguard Records, ‡c [1986], p1973.
300	‡a 1 sound disc (ca. 36 min.) : ‡b digital, stereo. ; ‡c 4 3/4 in.
538	‡a Compact disc.
500	‡a Title in distributor's catalog: Greatest hits.
511 0	‡a Joan Baez, vocals, with instrumental accompaniment.
505 0	‡a The night they drove old Dixie down / J. Robbie Robertson (3:22) -- Dangling conversation / Paul Simon (2:43) -- Help me make it through the night / Kris Kristofferson (2:58) -- Blessed are / Joan Baez (3:03) -- Eleanor Rigby / Paul McCartney, John Lennon (2:18) -- Let it be / Paul McCartney, John Lennon (3:48) -- There but for fortune / Phil Ochs (3:12) -- The brand new Tennessee waltz / Jesse Winchester (3:07) -- I pity the poor immigrant / Bob Dylan (3:45) -- Love is just a four-letter word / Bob Dylan (3:30) -- Heaven help us all / Ronald Miller (3:32).
650 8	‡a Popular music ‡z United States.
650 8	‡a Folk songs ‡z United States.
700 1	‡a Robertson, Jaime Robbie.
700 1	‡a Simon, Paul, ‡d 1941-
700 1	‡a Kristofferson, Kris.
700 1	‡a McCartney, Paul.
700 1	‡a Lennon, John, ‡d 1940-1980.
700 1	‡a Ochs, Phil.
700 1	‡a Winchester, Jesse.
700 1	‡a Dylan, Bob, ‡d 1941-
700 1	‡a Miller, Ron, ‡d 1941-
710 2	‡a Vanguard Records.

Note: If the slash mark in the 245 field causes a local system to think **Hits/greatest** is one word, not two, an <u>additional</u> 246 is needed substituting a space for the slash so that **Hits/greatest** can be found as two words. Some online systems see a slash or hyphen as a space; others ignore the slash or hyphen (like the apostrophe) and see the character string as continuous. Some systems even ignore ampersands, so that when an ampersand is included in a title search, the system will not find that title. Find out how the local system handles characters that are not letters or numbers.

Example of a CD by a musical group. The recording was previously released as both sound cassette and LP record. Main entry is under the performing group. There is no date on the item but it was possible to estimate a date. Members of the performing group are traced in 700 fields. Composers are also traced in 700 fields.

028 02 ‡a 1449-2 ‡b Warner Bros. Records

110 2 ‡a Peter, Paul, and Mary (Musical group)

245 10 ‡a Peter, Paul and Mary ‡h [sound recording].

260 ‡a Burbank, Calif. : ‡b Warner Bros. Records, Inc., ‡c [1988?]

300 ‡a 1 sound disc (34 min.) : ‡b digital ; ‡c 4 3/4 in. + ‡e program notes.

538 ‡a Compact disc.

511 0 ‡a Singers, Peter Yarrow, Paul Stookey, Mary Travers.

500 ‡a Previously released in 1962.

500 ‡a Program notes in booklet inserted in container.

520 ‡a Popular ballads; Peter, Paul and Mary accompanying themselves on guitar and cello.

505 0 ‡a Early in the morning / Paul Stookey (1:33) -- 500 miles / Hedy West (2:46) -- Sorrow / Stookey, Peter Yarrow (2:49) -- This train / Yarrow, Stookey (2:03) -- Bamboo / Dave Van Ronk (2:25) -- It's raining / Stookey, Yarrow (4:20) -- If I had my way / Gary Davis (2:17) -- Cruel war / Yarrow, Stookey (3:26) -- Lemon tree / Will Holt (2:52) -- If I had a hammer / Pete Seeger, Lee Hays (2:06) -- Autumn to May / Yarrow, Stookey (2:43) -- Where have all the flowers gone / Seeger (3:54).

650 8 ‡a Popular music ‡z United States.

650 8 ‡a Folk songs ‡z United States.

700 1 ‡a Yarrow, Peter, ‡d 1938-

700 1 ‡a Stookey, Paul, ‡d 1937-

700 1 ‡a Travers, Mary, ‡d 1936-

700 1 ‡a West, Hedy.

700 1 ‡a Van Ronk, Dave.

700 1 ‡a Davis, Gary, ‡d 1896-1972.

700 1 ‡a Holt, Will.

700 1 ‡a Seeger, Pete, ‡d 1919-

700 1 ‡a Hays, Lee, ‡d 1914-1981.

710 2 ‡a Warner Bros. Records.

Catalog card version:

Peter, Paul, and Mary (Musical group)
    Peter, Paul and Mary [sound recording]. -- Burbank, Calif. : Warner Bros. Records, Inc., [1988?]
    1 sound disc (34 min.) : digital ; 4 ¾ in. + program notes.

    Compact disc.
    Warner Bros. Records: 1449-2.
    Singers, Peter Yarrow, Paul Stookey, Mary Travers.
    Previously released in 1962.
    Program notes in booklet inserted in container.

 (Continued on next card)

Peter, Paul, and Mary (Musical group)
    Peter, Paul and Mary [sound recording] ... [1988?]   (Card 2)

    Summary: Popular ballads; Peter, Paul and Mary accompanying themselves on guitar and cello.
    Contents: Early in the morning / Paul Stookey (1:33) -- 500 miles / Hedy West (2:46) -- Sorrow / Stookey, Peter Yarrow (2:49) -- This train / Yarrow, Stookey (2:03) -- Bamboo / Van Ronk (2:25) -- It's raining / Stookey, Yarrow (4:20) -- If I had my way / Gary Davis (2:17) -- Cruel war / Yarrow, Stookey (3:26) -- Lemon tree / Will Holt (2:52) -- If I had a hammer / Seeger, Hayes (2:06) -- Autumn to May / Yarrow, Stookey (2:43) -- Where have all the flowers gone / Seeger (3:54).

 (Continued on next card)

Peter, Paul, and Mary (Musical group)
    Peter, Paul and Mary [sound recording] ... [1988?]   (Card 3)

    1. Popular music--United States. 2. Folk songs--United States. I. Yarrow, Peter, 1938-   II. Stookey, Paul, 1937-   III. Travers, Mary, 1936-   IV. West, Hedy. V. Van Ronk, Dave. VI. Davis, Gary, 1896-1972. VII. Holt, Will. VIII. Seeger, Pete, 1919- IX. Hays, Lee, 1914-1981. X. Warner Bros. Records. XI. Title.

Example of a two-volume CD featuring a jazz soloist with his musical group as backup. Main entry is under the soloist as the main performer.

028 02   ‡a G2K-40675 ‡b Columbia Records

100 1   ‡a Marsalis, Wynton, ‡d 1961-

245 14   ‡a The Wynton Marsalis Quartet live at Blues Alley ‡h [sound recording] / ‡c Wynton Marsalis.

246 30   ‡a Live at Blues Alley

260   ‡a New York, N.Y. : ‡b Columbia ; ‡a [Chicago, Ill. : ‡b Distributed by Rose Records], ‡c p1988.

300   ‡a 2 sound discs (107 min.) : ‡b digital ; ‡c 4 ¾ in. + ‡e 1 booklet (15 p. ; 12 cm.).

538   ‡a Compact disc.

511 0   ‡a Wynton Marsalis Quartet: Wynton Marsalis, trumpet ; Marcus Roberts, piano ; Robert Leslie Hurst III, bass ; Jeff "Tain" Watts, drums.

508   ‡a Producer, Steve Epstein.

518   ‡a Recorded on Dec. 19-20, 1986.

500   ‡a Copyright held by CBS Records Inc.

500   ‡a Program notes in booklet inserted in container.

520   ‡a Jazz music featuring Wynton Marsalis on the trumpet, accompanied by the rest of the Wynton Marsalis Quartet.

505 0   ‡a disc 1. Knozz-Moe-King (6:03) -- Just friends (8:22) -- Knozz-Moe-King (interlude) (3:53) -- Juan (7:33) -- Cherokee (2:51) -- Delfeayo's dilemma (9:13) -- Chambers of Tain (15:13) -- Juan (E. Mustaad) (2:56). disc 2. Au privave (14:35) -- Knozz-Moe-King (interlude) (2:38) -- Do you know what it means to miss New Orleans (11:31) -- Juan (Skip Mustaad) (3:15) -- Autumn leaves (9:42) -- Knozz-Moe-King (interlude) (3:48) -- Skain's domain (9:40) -- Much later (6:15).

650 8   ‡a Jazz music.

650 8   ‡a Jazz ensembles.

700 1   ‡a Roberts, Marcus.

700 1   ‡a Hurst, Bob.

700 1   ‡a Watts, Jeffrey.

700 1   ‡a Epstein, Steven.

710 2   ‡a Wynton Marsalis Quartet.

710 2   ‡a Columbia Records, Inc.

710 2   ‡a Rose Records.

710 2   ‡a CBS Records (Firm)

Example of a collection of Afro-American songs, recorded live at Carnegie Hall. Main entry is under performing group. Important singers are traced.

028 02	‡a FF 70106 ‡b Flying Fish Records, Inc.
110 2	‡a Sweet Honey in the Rock (Musical group)
245 10	‡a Live at Carnegie Hall ‡h [sound recording] / ‡c Sweet Honey in the Rock.
260	‡a Chicago, Ill. : ‡b Flying Fish Records, Inc., ‡c p1988.
300	‡a 1 sound disc (ca. 71 min.) : ‡b digital ; ‡c 4 ¾ in. + ‡e 1 folded sheet of lyrics.
538	‡a Compact disc.
511 0	‡a Sweet Honey in the Rock: singers, Bernice Johnson Reagon, Evelyn Maria Harris, Yasmeen Graham, Tulani Jordan-Kinard, Ysaye Maria Barnwell, Shirley Childress Johnson, Aisha Kahlil, Nitanju Bolade-Casel.
508	‡a Producers, Steve Rathe, Bernice Johnson Reagon.
518	‡a Recorded live in Carnegie Hall, Nov. 7, 1987.
500	‡a Folded sheet of lyrics inserted in container.
520	‡a Collection of Afro-American gospel songs and protest songs, performed by the musical group, Sweet Honey in the Rock.
505 0	‡a Beatitudes (3:50) -- Run, run, mourner run (5:10) -- Wade in the water (7:40) -- Drinking of the wine (3:45) -- Where are the keys to the kingdom? (2:28) -- Dream songs of love (7:27) -- Letter to Dr. Martin Luther King (8:05) -- Emergency (3:50) -- Our side won (5:20) -- Ode to the international debt (3:17) -- Are my hands clean? (3:03) -- Denko (4:40) -- My lament (3:42) -- Your worries ain' like mine (3:58) -- Song of the exiled (2:40) -- Peace (2:55).
650 8	‡a Gospel music.
650 8	‡a African American music.
700 1	‡a Reagon, Bernice Johnson, ‡d 1942-
700 1	‡a Harris, Evelyn M.
700 1	‡a Graham, Yasmeen.
700 2	‡a Jordan-Kinard, Tulani.
700 1	‡a Barnwell, Ysaye M.
700 1	‡a Johnson, Shirley Childress.
700 1	‡a Kahlil, Aisha.
700 2	‡a Bolade-Casel, Nitanju.
700 1	‡a Rathe, Steve.
710 2	‡a Flying Fish Records, Inc.

Example of a sound track of a musical on compact disc. Main entry is under first named composer. Title in 245 field is transcribed as stated on disc label (cannot be shortened to The king and I because of the possessive). Statement of Responsibility was prominent on Chief Source of Information (disc label).

028 02   ‡a RCD1-2610 ‡b RCA

100 1   ‡a Rodgers, Richard, ‡d 1902-

245 14   ‡a Rodgers & Hammerstein's The king and I ‡h [sound recording] / ‡c Yul Brynner and Broadway cast.

246 30   ‡a King and I

260   ‡a New York, N.Y. : ‡b RCA Red Seal, ‡c [198-?], p1977.

300   ‡a 1 sound disc (ca. 64 min.) : ‡b digital ; ‡c 4 ¾ in. + ‡e 1 booklet ([10] p. ; 12 cm.).

538   ‡a Compact disc.

511 1   ‡a Yul Brynner, Constance Towers, Hye-Young Choi, Martin Vidnovic, June Angela, Susan Kikuchi, John Michael King, Larry Swansen, Gene Profnato, Alan Amick, Rebecca West, Patricia Weber, Julie Woo, Michael Kermoyan.

508   ‡a Director, Yuriko ; musical director, Milton Rosenstock ; music, Richard Rodgers ; lyrics, Oscar Hammerstein 2nd.

500   ‡a Based on the novel: Anna and the King of Siam / Margaret Landon.

518   ‡a Recorded in RCA's Studio A, Oct. 31, 1977.

500   ‡a Musical compositions and dialogue, c1951.

500   ‡a Program notes in booklet inserted in container.

520   ‡a Music sound track from a stage performance of the musical by Richard Rodgers and Oscar Hammerstein.

505 0   ‡a Overture (5:04) -- Arrival at Bangkok / Men's Chorus ; I whistle a happy tune / Alan Amick, Constance Towers (3:27) -- My lord and master / June Angela (2:15) -- Hello, young lovers / Constance Towers (3:49) -- March of the Siamese children (3:27) -- Children sing, priests chant / Men's Chorus, Children's Chorus (0:47) -- A puzzlement / Yul Brynner (4:31) -- The Royal Bangkok Academy / Children's Chorus (0:44) -- Getting to know you / Constance Towers, Children's Chorus, Women's Chorus (4:23) -- So big a world / Yul Brynner (1:04) -- We kiss in a shadow / Martin Vidnovic, June Angela (4:12) -- A puzzlement (reprise) / Gene Profanato, Alan Amick (1:51) -- Shall I tell you what I think of you? / Constance Towers (5:28) -- Something wonderful / Hye-Young Choi (3:21) -- Finale to Act I / Company (2:31) -- Western people funny / Hye-Young Choi, Women's Chorus (1:35) -- Dance of Anna and Sir Edward (1:08) -- I have dreamed / Martin Vidnovic, June Angela (3:46) -- Song of the king / Yul Brynner, Constance Towers (1:12) -- Shall we dance? / Constance Towers, Yul Brynner (5:03) -- Finale / Constance Towers, Yul Brynner, Gene Profanato (6:06).

650 8   ‡a Musicals.

600 18   ‡a Leonowens, Anna Harriette, ‡d 1834-1914 ‡v Drama.

600 18   ‡a Mongkut, ‡c King of Siam, ‡d 1804-1868 ‡v Drama.

700 1   ‡a Hammerstein, Oscar, ‡d 1895-1960.

700 1   ‡a Brynner, Yul.

700 1   ‡a Towers, Constance.

700 1   ‡a Choi, Hye-Young.

700 1   ‡a Vidnovic, Martin.

700 1   ‡a Angela, June.

700 1   ‡a Amick, Alan.

700 0   ‡a Yuriko, ‡d 1920-

700 1   ‡a Rosenstock, Milton.

700 1   ‡a Landon, Margaret, ‡d 1903- ‡t Anna and the King of Siam.

710 2   ‡a RCA Red Seal (Firm)

Example of children's songs on sound cassette. There was no total duration on the item. Individual running times were not listed for songs.

245 00	‡a It takes two to sing ‡h [sound recording].
246 30	‡a Learning words through songs
260	‡a Toronto, Ont., Canada : ‡b Hanen Centre, ‡c c1995.
300	‡a 1 sound cassette : ‡b analog.
500	‡a Subtitle on container: Learning words through songs.
511 0	‡a Piano, Beth Knox ; vocals, Beth Knox, Colleen Graham, Mike Hughes.
508	‡a Producer, Beth Knox.
520	‡a Includes favorite children's songs that are sung very slowly, making it easy for children (even those with language delays) to sing along. Intended to promote language learning through song.
505 0	‡a side 1. Head and shoulders -- Old MacDonald -- Roll over -- Are you sleeping? -- Hokey Pokey -- My red train. side 2. I love you -- Monkey see -- Row, row, row your boat -- If you're happy -- This is the way -- Skinnamarink.
650 8	‡a Children's songs.
700 1	‡a Knox, Beth.
710 2	‡a Hanen Centre.

Example of children's songs on an LP record. Main entry is first named composer.

028 02	‡a PJ-1018 ‡b Sweet Punkin Productions
100 1	‡a Pascal, Peggy.
245 10	‡a Music is magic ‡h [sound recording] / ‡c Peggy Pascal, Jill Hearn.
246 3	‡a Musical learning experience for children
260	‡a Highland Park, IL : ‡b Sweet Punkin Productions, Inc., ‡c p1982.
300	‡a 1 sound disc (33 min.) : ‡b 33 1/3 rpm, stereo. ; ‡c 12 in. + ‡e 1 folded sheet of lyrics ([3] p. ; 30 x 30 cm.).
500	‡a Subtitle on container: A musical learning experience for children : colors, rhythms, animals, rhythm instruments, opposites, feelings, sharing and other good stuff.
511 0	‡a Musicians, Michelle Bailey, John Cummings, Bob Filler, Andrea Friederici, Claudia Friederici, Bob Golden, Mark Holmberg, James Gordon, Robert Lieberman, David Nelson, Peggy Pascal, Steve Roberts, Paul Schmidt, Jeff Urban, Paul Wertico ; vocalists, Peggy Pascal, Jill Hearn, Kerren Kalai, Marianne Katz, Michael Freeman ; with chorus of children ages 4-10.
508	‡a Producers/directors, Peggy Pascal, Jill Hearn.
500	‡a Accompanying lyrics sheet in container includes pattern for puppet and simple instructions on making homemade instruments.
521 8	‡a For ages 1-8.
520	‡a Original children's songs that encourage participation.
505 0	‡a side 1. Introduction -- Music is magic -- Opposites -- What do you do? -- Wiggle -- Let's go visit the zoo -- Sharing -- Colors. side 2. Let's build a body -- Anyday -- The rhyming game -- Rain -- I love to march -- Lullaby -- Conclusion.
650 8	‡a Children's songs.
650 8	‡a Singing games.
700 1	‡a Hearn, Jill.
710 2	‡a Sweet Punkin Productions.

Example of a collection of folk hymns on LP record. Subject heading Primitive Baptists **is borrowed from the Library of Congress but may be added as a Sears heading since it is the name of a religious denomination.**

020	‡a 0807840831
028 02	‡a 39088 ‡b American Folklore Recordings
245 00	‡a Primitive Baptist hymns of the Blue Ridge ‡h [sound recording] / ‡c recorded by Brett Sutton and Pete Hartman.
260	‡a Chapel Hill, N.C. : ‡b University of North Carolina Press, ‡c p1982.
300	‡a 1 sound disc (55 min.) : ‡b 33 1/3 rpm ; ‡c 12 in. + ‡e 1 booklet (27 p. : ill. ; 30 x 30 cm.).
440 0	‡a American folklore recordings
518	‡a Recorded at various Primitive Baptist churches in Virginia and North Carolina in 1976 as part of a documentary project in American folk religion.
500	‡a Contents and program notes on container.
504	‡a Booklet in container includes program notes by Brett Sutton, words of the hymns, musical transcription of some hymns, discography, and bibliographical references.
520	‡a Collection of unaccompanied traditional hymns from the Appalachian region.
505 0	‡a side 1. Dark was the night and cold the ground -- My God the spring of all my joys -- Poor and afflicted, Lord are thine -- 'Twas on that dark, that doleful night -- On Jordan's stormy banks I stand -- Jesus is a rock. side 2. I'm not ashamed to own my Lord -- Amazing grace, how sweet the sound -- Come thou long-expected Jesus -- I heard the voice of Jesus say -- Firmly I stand on Zion's hill -- Long sought home.
650 8	‡a Hymns.
650 8	‡a Folk songs ‡z Appalachian Region.
650 8	‡a Primitive Baptists ‡v Songs.
700 1	‡a Sutton, Brett.
700 1	‡a Hartman, Pete.
710 2	‡a University of North Carolina Press.

Example of a program on one side of a sound cassette, unrelated to the program on the other side and cataloged separately.

028 02	‡a HO-820104.02/10-C ‡b National Public Radio
245 00	‡a Gospel and spirituals ‡h [sound recording].
260	‡a Washington, D.C. : ‡b National Public Radio, ‡c p1982.
300	‡a 1 side of 1 sound cassette (28 min.) : ‡b analog.
511 0	‡a Host, Oscar Brown, Jr.
500	‡a Originally broadcast as a program on the educational television series: From Jumpstreet : a story of Black music / produced by WETA-TV.
500	‡a Jumpstreet television series is accompanied by curriculum guide: Jumpstreet humanities project : learning package : curriculum materials for secondary school teachers and students in language arts, history, and humanities.
520	‡a Examines the development and musical characteristics of spirituals and gospel music and relates the contemporary expression of these styles to their original functions and settings. Features Reverend James Cleveland and others.
501	‡a With: West African heritage.
650 8	‡a Gospel music ‡x History and criticism.
650 8	‡a Spirituals (Songs) ‡x History and criticism.
650 8	‡a African American music.
700 1	‡a Brown, Oscar.
700 1	‡a Cleveland, James.
710 2	‡a National Public Radio (U.S.)
710 2	‡a WETA-TV (Television station : Washington, D.C.)
730 0	‡a From Jumpstreet (Television program)
740 0	‡a Jumpstreet humanities project.

Example of a lecture on sound cassette. Main entry is under the speaker. No running time on item.

100 1		‡a Hayes, E. Kent, ‡d 1937-
245 10		‡a Perspectives on parenting ‡h [sound recording] / ‡c E. Kent Hayes.
260		‡a [Topeka, Kan.] : ‡b Menninger Management Institute, ‡c c1991.
300		‡a 1 sound cassette : ‡b analog.
440 0		‡a Life stages
520		‡a In a lecture, Kent Hayes shares some thoughts on what influences day-to-day roles as parents, and how to improve parenting skills to have happier, better-adjusted children. Developed from content presented at seminars.
650 8		‡a Parenting.
650 8		‡a Parent and child.
650 8		‡a Child rearing.
710 2		‡a Menninger Management Institute.

Example of a children's sound cassette with read-along book. Cassette is published by the author. The author is also the reader.

100 1	‡a Brown, Marc Tolon.
245 10	‡a Arthur goes to camp ‡h [sound recording] / ‡c by Marc Brown.
246 3	‡a Marc Brown reads Arthur
260	‡a [United States] : ‡b Marc Brown, ‡c p1994.
300	‡a 1 sound cassette (12 min.) : ‡b analog + ‡e 1 book ([32] p. : col. ill. ; 27 cm.).
500	‡a Distributor's title: Marc Brown reads Arthur.
511 0	‡a Reader, Marc Brown.
508	‡a Producer, Rosemary Killen.
500	‡a Includes theme song: Say hello to Arthur.
500	‡a Side 1 with turn-the-page signals; side 2 without signals.
500	‡a To be used with accompanying book of same title (Boston : Little, Brown and Co., c1982).
521 8	‡a For ages 4-8.
520	‡a Arthur is not looking forward to Camp Meadowcroak, and when mysterious things start happening there, he decides to run away.
650 8	‡a Animals ‡v Fiction.
650 8	‡a Camps ‡v Fiction.
650 8	‡a Talking books.
700 1	‡a Killen, Rosemary.

Example of an unabridged reading of a novel on sound cassette (multi-part item). Accent of reader is mentioned because reader is somewhat hard to understand at times.

028 02   ‡a 3CCA 3029 ‡b Chivers Audio Books

100 1   ‡a Howker, Janni.

245 14   ‡a The nature of the beast ‡h [sound recording] / ‡c by Janni Howker ; read by Christian Rodska.

260   ‡a [Bath, England] : ‡b Chivers Audio Books ; ‡a Boston, MA : ‡b G.K. Hall Audio Publishers [distributor], ‡c p1987.

300   ‡a 3 sound cassettes (221 min.) : ‡b analog.

440 0   ‡a Children's audio books

546   ‡a Read in a regional British accent.

520   ‡a Unabridged reading of the novel. Young Billy Coward's father and grandfather lose their jobs when the Haverston mill closes. Already ravaged by unemployment, Haverston is thrown into a state of fear by a mysterious beast which savagely kills livestock. Billy determines to track down the beast and kill it.

650 8   ‡a Adventure fiction.

650 8   ‡a Talking books.

700 1   ‡a Rodska, Christian.

710 2   ‡a Chivers Audio Books.

710 2   ‡a G.K. Hall Audio Publishers.

Example of an interview on sound cassette. Main entry is under the interviewee. No dimensions are given (no 300 ‡c) since cassette is standard size. Sears does not use the subject subdivision Interviews, **but the Library of Congress does.**

100 1	‡a Momaday, N. Scott, ‡d 1934-
245 10	‡a N. Scott Momaday interview ‡h [sound recording].
260	‡a [Columbia, Mo.] : ‡b American Audio Prose Library, ‡c [1983]
300	‡a 1 sound cassette (62 min.) : ‡b analog, mono.
518	‡a Recorded in Mar. 1983 at Momaday's home in Tucson, Ariz.
520	‡a Kay Bonetti interviews native American writer N. Scott Momaday. He discusses his Indian identity and heritage and its relationship to his writing.
600 10	‡a Momaday, N. Scott, ‡d 1934- ‡v Interviews.
650 8	‡a American literature ‡x American Indian authors.
700 1	‡a Bonetti, Kay.
710 2	‡a American Audio Prose Library.

Example of 4 programs from a radio series on a set of sound cassettes. Duration from container.

028 02   ‡a 41702T--41704T ‡b Radio Store

245 00   ‡a Breaking the cycle ‡h [sound recording] : ‡b how do we stop child abuse?

246 30   ‡a How do we stop child abuse?

246 3   ‡a Breaking the cycle : ‡b what you can do to help stop child abuse

246 3   ‡a What you can do to help stop child abuse

260   ‡a [Madison, Wis.] : ‡b Radio Store, ‡c c1994.

300   ‡a 4 sound cassettes (ca. 60 min. each) : ‡b analog. + ‡e 1 information sheet.

500   ‡a Title on container spine: Breaking the cycle : what you can do to help stop child abuse.

511 0   ‡a Hosts, Susan Stamberg, Alex Chadwick.

508   ‡a Producers, Dan Gediman, Jay Allison.

500   ‡a Copyright held by Milestone Productions.

500   ‡a Sound cassette version of a four-part national call-in program from National Public Radio.

500   ‡a Program notes on container.

520   ‡a Designed to educate individuals on how to recognize child abuse and neglect, and also on how to put a stop to it. Each program features stories about people and institutions that have either found ways to use existing programs and structures to better serve abused and neglected children, or who have paved new paths when they have found the status quo either ineffective or dangerous for children. Discussions with experts on child abuse follow each feature. Program 1 features stories on two child abuse programs in the United States: Healthy Families America and Parents Anonymous. Reports on the relationship between substance abuse and child abuse and neglect. Program 2 looks at the experience of Sweden, which outlawed physical punishment of children; interviews Joyce Thomas of the People of Color Leadership Institute; and explores the work of the Northwest Indian Child Welfare Institute. Program 3 documents approaches for preventing child sexual abuse that are being used in classrooms, churches, homes, and community settings, and interviews Cordelia Anderson, a pioneer in the field. Program 4 includes interviews with U.S. Rep. Pat Schroeder and Jeanne Lenzer, national chairperson of the National Child Rights Alliance.

505 0   ‡a program 1. Helping parents -- program 2. The role of culture in preventing child abuse -- program 3. Preventing child sexual abuse -- program 4. Shaping future public policy.

650 8   ‡a Child abuse.

650 8   ‡a Child sexual abuse.

650 8   ‡a Parenting.

610 28   ‡a Healthy Families America (Program)

610 28   ‡a Parents Anonymous (U.S.)

610 28   ‡a Northwest Indian Child Welfare Institute.

700 1   ‡a Stamberg, Susan, ‡d 1938-

700 1 ‡a Chadwick, Alex, ‡d 1947-

700 1 ‡a Gediman, Dan.

700 1 ‡a Allison, Jay.

700 1 ‡a Thomas, Joyce N.

700 1 ‡a Anderson, Cordelia.

700 1 ‡a Schroeder, Pat.

700 1 ‡a Lenzer, Jeanne.

710 2 ‡a Radio Store.

710 2 ‡a Milestone Productions (Firm)

710 2 ‡a National Public Radio (U.S.)

Example of a radio program on sound cassette, readings from the works of several poets with commentary. Cassette series has part numbers and appears in 440, as well as in 730 as a radio program. The poets are both added entries and subject headings because the recording contains readings from their works as well as commentary about them.

028 02   ‡a ME-801210.06.12-C ‡b National Public Radio

245 00   ‡a Modern American poets. ‡n Segment A ‡h [sound recording].

260   ‡a [Washington, D.C.] : ‡b National Public Radio, ‡c p1980.

300   ‡a 1 sound cassette (55 min.) : ‡b analog.

440 0   ‡a Morning edition series ; ‡v pt. 6

500   ‡a Sound cassette version of a segment from the NPR radio program, Morning edition.

520   ‡a Readings from the works of several American poets, along with commentary on their lives and works. Includes Emily Dickinson, Adrienne Rich, James Russell Lowell, Amy Lowell, and Wallace Stevens.

650 8   ‡a American poets.

650 8   ‡a American poetry ‡x History and criticism.

600 18   ‡a Dickinson, Emily, ‡d 1830-1886.

600 18   ‡a Rich, Adrienne Cecile.

600 18   ‡a Lowell, James Russell, ‡d 1819-1891.

600 18   ‡a Lowell, Amy, ‡d 1874-1925.

600 18   ‡a Stevens, Wallace, ‡d 1879-1955.

700 1   ‡a Dickinson, Emily, ‡d 1830-1886.

700 1   ‡a Rich, Adrienne Cecile.

700 1   ‡a Lowell, James Russell, ‡d 1819-1891.

700 1   ‡a Lowell, Amy, ‡d 1874-1925.

700 1   ‡a Stevens, Wallace, ‡d 1879-1955.

710 2   ‡a National Public Radio (U.S.)

730 0   ‡a Morning edition (Radio program)

Example of a comedy radio program on sound cassette. There was no publication or copyright date on item. Date is a guess at the decade.

028 02   ‡a 516 ‡b Old Time Radio

245 00   ‡a Fibber McGee & Molly ‡h [sound recording].

246 3   ‡a Fibber McGee and Molly

260   ‡a Denver, Colo. : ‡b Old Time Radio, ‡c [197-?]

300   ‡a 1 sound cassette (61 min.) : ‡b analog.

520   ‡a Two 1945 episodes from the comedy radio program, Fibber McGee & Molly.

505 0   ‡a side 1. Brief Case Bronson, 5/1/45 (31 min.) -- side 2. Mrs. Carstairs, 6/19/45 (30 min.).

650 8   ‡a Radio programs.

650 8   ‡a Comedy radio programs.

710 2   ‡a Old Time Radio.

730 0   ‡a Fibber McGee & Molly (Radio program)

740 02   ‡a Brief Case Bronson.

740 02   ‡a Mrs. Carstairs.

Example of a collection of comedy radio broadcasts by W. C. Fields. Main entry under performer.

028 02   ‡a BT 22260 ‡b Sony Music Entertainment

100 1   ‡a Fields, W. C., ‡d 1879-1946.

245 14   ‡a The best of W.C. Fields ‡h [sound recording].

260   ‡a [New York, N.Y.] : ‡b Sony Music Entertainment, Inc., ‡c [1991], p1976.

300   ‡a 2 sound cassettes (103 min.) : ‡b analog, mono.

500   ‡a Most selections previously released in 1976 as LP records, Columbia CGT 34144.

520   ‡a Radio broadcasts of comedy routines by W.C. Fields, some alone and some with supporting comedians Don Ameche and Edgar Bergen (with puppet Charlie McCarthy).

505 0   ‡a vol. 1 (58 min.): Promotions unlimited / W.C. Fields -- The temperance lecture / Fields -- Communing with nature / Fields with Edgar Bergen, Charlie McCarthy, & Don Ameche -- The snake story (A commercial) / Fields with Ameche -- The pharmacist / Fields -- Father's Day / Fields with Bergen, McCarthy, & Ameche.   vol. 2 (45 min.): The golf game / Fields with Bergen, McCarthy, & Ameche -- The skunk trap / Fields with Bergen & McCarthy -- Tales of Michael Finn, a tender ballad / Fields -- Strike up the band (a Fieldsian commercial) / Fields -- Fire in the house / Fields -- Romeo & Juliet / Fields with Bergen, McCarthy, & Ameche -- The purple bark sarsaparilla pitch / Fields.

650 8   ‡a Radio programs.

650 8   ‡a Comedy radio programs.

700 1   ‡a Ameche, Don.

700 1   ‡a Bergen, Edgar, ‡d 1903-1978.

710 2   ‡a Sony Music Entertainment, Inc.

Example of a collection of sound effects on compact disc. Form of series on item differs from authorized form of the series title.

028 02 ‡a BBC CD SFX039 Films for the Humanities & Sciences

245 00 ‡a Schools and crowds ‡h [sound recording].

246 3 ‡a Schools/crowds

260 ‡a Princeton, N.J. : ‡b Films for the Humanities & Sciences, ‡c c1991.

300 ‡a 1 sound disc (ca. 62 min.) : ‡b digital, stereo. ; ‡c 4 ¾ in. + ‡e 1 contents list (1 folded sheet) + 1 series guide (76 p. ; 28 cm.).

490 1 ‡a BBC sound effects library ; ‡v 39

538 ‡a Compact disc.

500 ‡a Title from container.

500 ‡a Title on container spine: Schools/crowds.

500 ‡a Copyright held by BBC Enterprises.

518 ‡a Recorded in Great Britain.

520 ‡a Part of a series of 40 volumes of sound effects. This segment is a field recording of school sounds and crowd sounds. School sounds include hall, classroom, playground, girls' changing room, sports hall (basketball), computer class, and gym class. Crowd sounds include indoor market, dinner dance, public house, and hall.

650 8 ‡a Sound effects.

650 8 ‡a Sounds.

650 8 ‡a Schools.

650 8 ‡a Crowds.

710 2 ‡a Films for the Humanities (Firm)

710 2 ‡a BBC Enterprises.

830 0 ‡a Sound effects ; ‡v 39.

Example of a spoken recording on an LP record. There are several short segments, listed in the 505 Contents Note. In personal name headings, Jr. is not usually included when dates are known, but the Library of Congress made an exception in this case.

028 02   ‡a SR61203 ‡b Mercury Record Productions

245 04   ‡a The sound of dissent ‡h [sound recording].

260   ‡a Chicago, Ill. : ‡b Mercury Record Productions, ‡c [1970?]

300   ‡a 1 sound disc (31 min.) : ‡b analog, 33 1/3 rpm, stereo. ; ‡c 12 in.

500   ‡a Producer, Jack McMahon ; music, Dan Armstrong.

500   ‡a Program notes on container.

520   ‡a Excerpts from recorded comments by newsworthy participants in various protest movements of the 1960s: civil rights, the antiwar movement, women's rights, etc. Recorded on-site as these events took place.

505 0   ‡a side 1. Intro. (2:37) -- Poor people's Campaign, Supreme Court Bldg., Wash., D.C. (3:33) -- Anti-draft remarks (3:00) -- Peace March, Wash., D.C. and New York (4:14) -- Loyalty Day Parade, New York (2:44). side 2. Anti-war march, New York and Wash., D.C. (2:30) -- Democratic National Convention, Chicago (5:28) -- Campus (1:30) -- Women protest (1:45) -- Martin Luther King (0:55) -- Eulogy (2:55).

650 8   ‡a Demonstrations ‡z United States.

651 8   ‡a United States ‡x History ‡y 1961-1974.

650 8   ‡a Vietnam War, 1961-1975 ‡x Protest movements.

650 8   ‡a African Americans ‡x Civil rights.

600 18   ‡a King, Martin Luther, ‡c Jr., ‡d 1929-1968.

700 1   ‡a McMahon, Jack.

710 2   ‡a Mercury Record Productions.

CHAPTER 8
CATALOGING COMPUTER SOFTWARE

AACR2R Rules for Computer Software

Use Chapter 9 in AACR2R for computer software, along with general rules in Chapter 1. In schools, most computer software will be floppy disks or CD-ROM discs. Some libraries are now cataloging Internet resources, but there is debate about the feasibility of spending the cataloging time, since Internet databases come and go without warning. Computer software that meets the criteria for interactive multimedia is governed by a different set of cataloging rules (see Chapter 9 in this book).

Chief Source of Information

The Chief Source of Information is the title screen. If at all possible, boot up the program, make sure it works properly, and look at the title screen and other preliminary screens. In addition to the title, other information may also be on these screens, such as programmers, authors, edition, and date. If it is not possible to boot up the program, AACR2R rules allow the cataloger to use the eye-readable label on the disk/disc as the Chief Source of Information. If there is no label, take the title from the following in this order: documentation issued with the computer file, or the container.

Title (245 ‡a and ‡b)

Use the title screen title as the Title Proper if possible. If it is not possible to see the title screen, use the title on the disk/disc label. A 500 Source of Title note is required for computer software. If the title varies on the title screen, disk label, documentation, container, or in the distributor's catalog, make 500 notes listing the title variations and trace them in 246 fields, as for other formats.

GMD (245 ‡h)

Regardless of the physical format (computer disk, CD-ROM disc, Internet database, etc.), the GMD for computer files is currently **[computer file]**. Computer software that meets the guidelines for interactive multimedia uses the GMD **[interactive multimedia]**. However, the newest version of the *ISBD(ER): International Standard Bibliographic Description for Electronic Resources*, now almost through the approval process, is expected to replace the GMDs **[computer file]** and **[interactive multimedia]** with the more generic **[electronic resource]**. Watch for word of an official change in the near future. Until then, use **[computer file]** or **[interactive multimedia]**. The entire ISBD(ER) document may be accessed at: http://www.ifla.org/VII/s13/pubs/isbd.htm.

Statement of Responsibility (245 ‡c)

If the cataloger is unable to view the title screen, but must find names of responsible persons on the container or in accompanying documentation, there will be no Statement of Responsibility. Such information found outside the Chief Source of Information should be transcribed in a 508 Credits Note.

Edition Statement (250 field)

This may be similar to the Edition Statement for a book, or it may be the version of the program. Examples:

250   ‡a Version 5.20.
250   ‡a Windows version.

Unlike other nonbook formats, computer software will usually have some kind of Edition Statement on the disk/disc or accompanying material. If so, be sure to include it so that there is no confusion with other versions. Computer software is frequently upgraded.

Computer File Characteristics (256 field)

The 256 field, Computer File Characteristics, is defined as mandatory for computer software. But in practice, most catalogers do not use the 256 field except for Internet resources (if the information is known). The Library of Congress does not use the 256 field. If a cataloger wishes to use it, here are some examples:

256   ‡a Computer program (2 files).
256   ‡a Computer data (2 files : 800, 1250 records) and programs (3 files : 7260, 3490, 5076 bytes).
256   ‡a Computer data and programs.

In the newest version of the **ISBD(ER): International Standard Bibliographic Description for Electronic Resources**, the 256 field (Area 3) shows several examples of more specific descriptions. These new descriptions will identify specific types of computer software early in the bibliographic description, rather than in 5XX notes that may not appear on the "brief view" screen in an online catalog.

Physical Description Area (300 field)

See examples in AACR2. In the 300 field, floppy disks will be described like the following:

300   ‡a 1 computer disk : ‡b col. ; ‡c 3 1/2 in. + ‡e 1 manual (51 p. : ill. ; 20 cm.).
300   ‡a 1 computer disk ; ‡c 3 1/2 in. + ‡e 1 demonstration disk + 1 codebook (16 p. ; 16 cm.).
300   ‡a 2 computer disks ; ‡c 5 1/4 in.
        (in Note Area, add explanatory 500 notes, e.g.: **Second disk is backup.**)

A CD computer file will be described like the following in the 300 field:

300   ‡a 1 computer optical disc : ‡b col. ; ‡c 4 3/4 in. + ‡e 1 guide (36 p. ; 28 cm.).

Until recently, CD computer files were designated as **computer <u>laser</u> optical discs** in the Physical Description field, and many older cataloging records use **laser**. AACR2R originally required the spelling **disk** for CD computer software (as opposed to **disc** for sound compact discs). A recent AACR2 rule revision has officially established **disc** for CD computer files. Floppies are still **disk**.

Sound or color features are recorded in 300 ‡b. The color feature is similar to physical description of books: **col.** is recorded when appropriate, but if the item is in black-and-white, 300 ‡b is omitted if **sd.** is not needed.

When cataloging Internet resources, omit the 300 field since the computer file is not a physical item in hand.

Notes (5XX fields)

The first note is a 538 System Requirements Note. Precede the note with **System requirements:** (not a print constant). This note helps the user determine what equipment is necessary to use the software. If any of the following information is on the software, accompanying documentation, or container, include it in the following order in the 538 note, separated by semicolon-space:

Make/model of computer on which the software is designed to run
Amount of memory required/recommended
Name of operating system
Software requirements, including programming language
Kind and characteristics of required or recommended peripherals

The next note is mandatory for all computer software: a 500 Source of Title Note telling the source of the Title Proper: e.g.: **Title from disk label.** or **Title from title screen.** For other nonbook formats, use such a note only when the title comes from outside the Chief Source of Information.

Cataloging records for computer software should have a 520 Summary Note. If there are separate parts, a 505 Contents Note is needed.

Subject Headings and Added Entries (6XX and 7XX fields)

Use subject headings that would be appropriate if the item were a book. Some libraries add the form subdivision ‡v **Computer programs** to subject headings for computer software. This is a local policy decision, but as defined by the Library of Congress, **Computer programs** is for the actual programming code, not the end product (software). For computer software, school libraries can borrow the LC form subdivision ‡v **Software** to add to topical subject headings (see examples later in this chapter).

Do not use the Sears subject heading or subject subdivision **Computer assisted instruction** unless the item is about this type of instruction (not if it is this type of instruction). Do not use the topical subject heading **Computer software** just because the item is a piece of software. This subject heading is intended only for items about computer software. Do not use the topical subject heading **Computer games** for a computer disc that is a computer game, but only for software about computer games. For computer games, a local option is to borrow the Library of Congress form subdivision ‡v **Computer games** to subdivide subjects.

Added entries are as for other types of nonbook materials. Trace responsible persons and corporate bodies, including publishers.

Examples follow.

145

Example of a floppy disk. This is a cartographic program. The publishing company is the main entry according to the rules for main entry for cartographic materials. Typography indicated a need for the variant title in the 246 field (space between Mac and Globe). Subjects are subdivided by borrowing the LC form subdivision Software.

110 2 ‡a PC Globe, Inc.

245 10 ‡a MacGlobe ‡h [computer file] : ‡b electronic atlas for the Macintosh computer.

246 30 ‡a Mac Globe : ‡b electronic atlas for the Macintosh computer

250 ‡a Version 1.0.

260 ‡a Tempe, Ariz. : ‡b PC Globe, Inc. ; ‡a [Lakewood, N.J. : ‡b Distributed by MacWarehouse], ‡c c1991.

300 ‡a 2 computer disks : ‡b col. ; ‡c 3 1/2 in. + ‡e 1 user's guide (38 p. : ill. ; 22 cm.).

538 ‡a System requirements: Macintosh Plus or later model; at least 1 MB RAM; Macintosh System 6.0.4 or later, including 7.0; hard disk; single 800K disk drive.

500 ‡a Title from disk label.

520 ‡a Includes regional maps for the world, Africa, Asia, Australia and Oceania, Europe, North America, South America, Central America, the Middle East, and Southeast Asia, and 190 country maps. Allows modification of maps by painting countries and regions, displaying cities, and adding map features. Includes statistical data on demographics, health, economics, education, electricity, coal, natural gas, crude petroleum, mining, agriculture, and manufacturing.

650 8 ‡a Maps ‡v Software.

650 8 ‡a Atlases ‡v Software.

650 8 ‡a Almanacs ‡v Software.

710 2 ‡a MacWarehouse (Firm)

Catalog card version:

PC Globe, Inc.
    MacGlobe [computer file] : electronic atlas for the Macintosh computer. -- Version 1.0. -- Tempe, Ariz. : PC Globe, Inc. ; [Lakewood, N.J. : Distributed by MacWarehouse], c1991.
    2 computer disks : col. ; 3 ½ in. + 1 user's guide (38 p. : ill. ; 22 cm.).

    System requirements: Macintosh Plus or later model; at least 1 MB RAM; Macintosh System 6.0.4 or later, including 7.0; hard disk; single 800K disk drive.
    Title from disk label.

 (Continued on next card)

PC Globe, Inc.
    MacGlobe [computer file] ... c1991.   (Card 2)

    Summary: Includes regional maps for the world, Africa, Asia, Australia and Oceania, Europe, North America, South America, Central America, the Middle East, and southeast Asia, and 190 country maps. Allows modification of maps by painting countries and regions, displaying cities, and adding map features. Includes statistical data on demographics, health, economics, education, electricity, coal, natural gas, crude petroleum, mining, agriculture, and manufacturing.

 (Continued on next card)

PC Globe, Inc.
    MacGlobe [computer file] ... c1991.   (Card 3)

    1. Maps--Software. 2. Atlases--Software. 3. Almanacs--Software. I. MacWarehouse (Firm) II. Title: Mac Globe : electronic atlas for the Macintosh computer.

Example of an electronic book on floppy disk. The second subject heading is borrowed from the Library of Congress.

100 1	‡a Melville, Herman, ‡d 1819-1891.
245 10	‡a Moby Dick ‡h [computer file] / ‡c Herman Melville.
260	‡a Santa Monica, CA : ‡b Voyager Co., ‡c c1992.
300	‡a 2 computer disks ; ‡c 3 1/2 in. + ‡e 1 installation leaflet + 1 information sheet.
440 0	‡a Voyager expanded book
538	‡a System requirements: Macintosh PowerBook or any Macintosh large display (640 x 400 or greater); 2 MB RAM; System 6.0.7 or later; HyperCard 2.1 or later; hard drive.
500	‡a Title from disk label.
520	‡a Electronic book with full text of Melville's classic novel about Captain Ahab and his obsessive quest for the great white whale. Reproduces the illustrations and page design created by Rockwell Kent for Random House in 1930. Program allows interaction with the text, such as searching for words and phrases.
650 8	‡a Whaling ‡x Fiction.
650 0	‡a Electronic books.
700 1	‡a Kent, Rockwell, ‡d 1882-1971.
710 2	‡a Voyager Company.
710 2	‡a Random House (Firm)

Example of a CD-ROM computer disc. The second 246 would be used for systems that see a hyphen as a space. It would be a duplication of the 245 title for systems that ignore hyphens and pull the character string together. Little information on system requirements was provided on or with the item. Two Library of Congress subject headings are included, since there are no corresponding Sears headings.

245 00   ‡a CD7 ‡h [computer file] : ‡b Mac CD-ROM library : a unique super-library of public domain and shareware files for the Macintosh.

246 30   ‡a Mac CD-ROM library

246 3   ‡a CD-7

260   ‡a Coral Gables, FL : ‡b QLTech ; ‡a Louisville, KY : ‡b Ztek Co. [distributor], ‡c c1990.

300   ‡a 1 computer optical disc ; ‡c 4 3/4 in.

538   ‡a System requirements: Macintosh computer; Hypercard; CD-ROM player.

500   ‡a Title from disc label.

500   ‡a Title in distributor's catalog: CD-7.

500   ‡a "HSF format."

520   ‡a CD-ROM collection of public domain and shareware files for the Macintosh (over 700 megabytes). Includes 2,570 art files, 931 games, 828 HyperCard stacks, 1,262 demo files, 1,180 digitized sounds, and 1,453 music files.

650 8   ‡a Macintosh (Computer) ‡v Computer programs.

650 0   ‡a Shareware (Computer software)

650 0   ‡a Free computer software.

710 2   ‡a Quantum Leap Technologies, Inc.

710 2   ‡a Ztek Co.

Example of a children's educational computer program on floppy disks.

245 00	‡a Muppetville ‡h [computer file].
250	‡a Macintosh ed.
260	‡a Pleasantville, NY : ‡b Sunburst Communications, Inc., ‡c c1995.
300	‡a 2 computer disks : ‡b sd., col. ; ‡c 3 1/2 in. + ‡e 1 teacher's guide (78 leaves : ill. ; 30 cm.).
538	‡a System requirements: Color Macintosh with sound; 4 MB; 1.4 MB disk drive; System 6.0.5 or greater.
500	‡a Title from disk label.
500	‡a Produced by Jim Henson Productions and Sunburst Communications, Inc.
511 0	‡a Voices, Frank Oz, Steve Whitmire, Dave Goetz, Jerry Nelson.
508	‡a Project managers, Debra Weinberger, Eleanor Arita ; original design, Christopher Cerf, Bill Prady, Marge Cappo, Mike Fish, Melissa Verber ; teacher's guide, Raoul Watson, Joni Jablansky ; editor, Emilie Rappoport ; graphics and programming, Raoul Watson.
521 8	‡a For preschool through first grade and special education.
520	‡a Activities in discriminating shapes, size, color, and musical tones; determining likeness and difference among objects; counting and adding.
505 0	‡a Animal's apartment house -- Sam the Eagle's school -- Muppet factory -- The Statler Waldorf Hotel -- Gonzo's zoo -- Muppet movies.
650 8	‡a Size ‡v Software.
650 8	‡a Shape ‡v Software.
650 8	‡a Color ‡v Software.
650 8	‡a Music ‡x Study and teaching ‡v Software.
650 8	‡a Counting ‡v Software.
650 8	‡a Arithmetic ‡x Study and teaching ‡v Software.
650 8	‡a Educational games.
700 1	‡a Oz, Frank.
700 1	‡a Cerf, Christopher.
700 1	‡a Watson, Raoul.
710 2	‡a Sunburst Communications (Firm)
710 2	‡a Jim Henson Productions.
740 02	‡a Animal's apartment house.
740 02	‡a Sam the Eagle's school.
740 02	‡a Muppet factory.
740 02	‡a Statler Waldorf Hotel.
740 02	‡a Gonzo's zoo.
740 02	‡a Muppet movies.

CD-ROM disc for either Windows or Macintosh. There are two 538 fields. The ‡v form subdivision Computer games is borrowed from the Library of Congress.

020	‡a 0792908872 (guide)
037	‡a CD606 ‡b MECC
245 04	‡a The Oregon Trail ‡h [computer file] : ‡b CD-ROM for Windows or Macintosh.
246 3	‡a Oregon Trail CD
250	‡a Version 1.0.
260	‡a Minneapolis, Minn. : ‡b MECC, ‡c c1994.
300	‡a 1 computer optical disc : ‡b sd., col. ; ‡c 4 ¾ in. + ‡e 1 manual (45 p. ; 30 cm.) + 1 information sheet.
538	‡a System requirements: Macintosh computer; 4 MB RAM; System 7.0 or later; hard disk; color monitor; CD-ROM drive.
538	‡a System requirements: Windows-compatible computer 80386 CPU or higher; 4 MB RAM; MS-DOS 5.0 or later; Windows 3.1; hard disk; SVGA color monitor (256 colors); CD-ROM drive; Windows-compatible sound card.
500	‡a Title from disc label.
500	‡a Title on manual: The Oregon Trail CD.
521 8	‡a For grades 5-12, ages 10-adult.
520	‡a Educational simulation game designed to develop social studies skills as students travel by covered wagon on an 1848 journey from Independence, Mo., to the Willamette Valley of Oregon. Players relive the days of pioneers as they hunt buffalo, raft down rivers, and make many important survival decisions while moving their families across the frontier. Playing time is at least 25 min. for individuals, longer for groups.
651 8	‡a Oregon Trail ‡v Computer games.
650 8	‡a Frontier and pioneer life ‡v Computer games.
650 8	‡a Educational games.
710 2	‡a Minnesota Educational Computing Corporation.

Example of a collection of books, pamphlets, and articles on CD-ROM, for either IBM or Macintosh.

245 00 ‡a History of the world ‡h [computer file] : ‡b a complete and authoritative world history reference on CD-ROM.

246 3 ‡a History of the world on CD-ROM

260 ‡a Parsippany, NJ : ‡b Bureau Development, Inc., ‡c c1992.

300 ‡a 1 computer optical disc : ‡b sd., col. ; ‡c 4 ¾ in. + ‡e 1 manual.

490 1 ‡a Library reference series

538 System requirements: IBM PC/XT/AT or PS/2; 640K; DOS 3.1 or later; Microsoft extensions 2.0 or later; VGA board and monitor; CD-ROM drive; hard disk, speakers or headphones, printer recommended.

538 System requirements: Macintosh Plus/SE/SE-30/II/Classic/LC; 300K space on hard disk; 1 MB RAM; system software 6.0.4 or greater; other peripherals as on IBM.

500 ‡a Title from disc label.

500 ‡a Title on t.p. of manual: History of the world on CD-ROM.

520 ‡a Books, pamphlets and articles on world history compiled on a CD-ROM database. Users can search words, authors, subjects, titles, or pictures.

650 8 ‡a World history ‡v Software.

650 8 ‡a Civilization ‡x History ‡v Software.

710 2 ‡a Bureau Development, Inc.

830 0 ‡a Library reference series (Parsippany, N.J.)

Example of a CD-ROM disc with pictures that may be copied to create written documents and presentations. Accompanied by printed materials and another CD-ROM disc. One subject heading is borrowed from the Library of Congress since there is no comparable Sears subject heading.

245 00   ‡a Corel gallery for Macintosh ‡h [computer file] : ‡b 10,000 clipart images : add flair to your word processing and presentations.

246 30   ‡a Gallery for Macintosh

246 30   ‡a 10,000 clipart images

246 30   ‡a Ten thousand clipart images

246 3   ‡a Corel gallery

250   ‡a Version 1.0.

260   ‡a Ottawa, Ont., Canada : ‡b Corel Corp. ; ‡a Louisville, Ky. : ‡b Ztek Co. [distributor], ‡c c1994.

300   ‡a 1 computer optical disc : ‡b col. ; ‡c 4 ¾ in. + ‡e 1 reference manual (344 p. : col. ill. ; 23 cm.) + 1 quickstart guide + 1 computer optical disc sampler + 1 sampler guide.

538   ‡a System requirements: Macintosh computer with MC68020 processor or later; at least 4 MB (8 MB or more recommended, especially if using Photo CD images); System 7.0 or later; color QuickDraw; Quicktime 1.6.1 or later (for preview decompression); CD-ROM drive.

500   ‡a Title in distributor's catalog: Corel gallery.

500   ‡a Accompanied by computer optical disc: Sampler : Corel professional photos CD-ROM. Limited ed., version 1.00. c1993.

500   ‡a Accompanying reference manual shows images on the disc divided by category. Sampler guide shows col. photographs on Sampler disc.

520   ‡a CD-ROM file containing 10,000 professionally-drawn images and 100 royalty-free photos in Kodak photo CD format. Works with Macintosh word processing applications (ClarisWorks, Word, MacWrite II/Pro), presentation and graphics (Deneba canvas, FreeHand, MacDraw pro, IntelliDraw, Persuasion); and publishing (PageMaker, QuarkXpress, Personal Press).

505 0   ‡a Portraits -- 3D -- Aircraft -- Animals -- Arrows -- Awards -- Birds -- Business -- Celebrations -- Charts -- Children -- Communication -- Computers -- Crests -- Crustaceans -- Designs -- Electronics -- Fantasy -- Fires -- Fish -- Flags -- Food -- Holiday -- Homes -- Insects -- Insignias -- Justice -- Landmarks -- Leisure -- Men -- Maps -- Medical -- Miscellaneous -- Money -- Music -- People/Business -- People/Humor -- People/Icon -- People/Misc. -- Plants -- Reptiles -- Ships -- Signs -- Simple borders -- Space -- Sports -- Theme borders -- Tools -- Vehicles -- Weapons -- Weather -- Women.

650 8   ‡a Clip art ‡v Software.

650 8   ‡a Desktop publishing ‡v Software.

710 2   ‡a Corel Corporation.

710 2   ‡a Ztek Co.

740 02   ‡a Sampler, Corel professional photos CD-ROM.

740 02   ‡a Corel professional photos CD-ROM.

Example of a collection of film clips on CD-ROM. The 520 Summary Note is constructed to aid keyword search. This program has some features of interactive multimedia (use of Hypercard and Quicktime) but navigation is linear.

037		‡a MM1000 ‡b MPI Multimedia
245 04		‡a The archives of history ‡h [computer file] : ‡b a moving-image retrospective of the 20th century.
246 30		‡a Moving-image retrospective of the 20th century
260		‡a Oak Forest, Ill. : ‡b MPI Multimedia, ‡c c1993.
300		‡a 1 computer optical disc : ‡b sd., col. ; ‡c 4 ¾ in. + ‡e 1 user's guide (14 p. ; 12 x 12 cm.) + 1 information sheet.
440 0		‡a WPA multimedia collection
538		‡a System requirements: Macintosh LC III or faster; at least 3 MB free RAM; System 7 or later; Hypercard; Quicktime (on disc); hard drive; minimum 256 color graphics (16- or 24-bit graphics recommended); double-speed CD-ROM drive or faster.
500		‡a Title from disc label.
500		‡a Film clips from the library of the Work Projects Administration.
508		‡a Executive producers, Waleed B. Ali, Malik B. Ali ; series producer, Lou Zucaro ; software design/programming, Lou Zucaro ; writing, Sean McGinty.
520		‡a Multimedia/Hypercard collection of over 250 moving picture clips from pre-1900 to 1993. Events: Hindenberg explosion; repeal of prohibition; Titanic distater, Klan march on Washington; Lindbergh arrives in Paris; stock market crash, 1929; Army-McCarthy hearings; Watergate; King Tut's tomb excavated; Bruno Hauptmann electrocuted; Jackie Robinson joins the Brooklyn Dodgers; Dionne quintuplets. Wars: World War I; World War II; Russian Revolution; Boer War; Vietnam; Korea; Spanish Civil War; Easter Rebellion; Cold War; Desert Storm; Nuremberg Trials; Atomic blast over Hiroshima; Yalta Conference; anti-war demonstrations; kamikazes; Pearl Harbor; Elvis Presley inducted into the Army. Personalities: George Bernard Shaw, Amelia Earhart, John F. Kennedy, Adolph Hitler, Thomas Edison, Sir Edmund Hillary, Henry Ford, Benito Mussolini, Mohandas Gandhi, Marilyn Monroe, Gamal Abdal Nasser, Vladimir Ilyich Lenin, Richard Nixon, John Dillinger, Franklin Delano Roosevelt, Josef Stalin, Twiggy, Will Rogers, Charles Lindbergh, Martin Luther King, Jr. Lifestyles: Depression America; gangsters; flappers; hula hoops; marathon dancing; families with televisions; swingin' London; voter registration drives; fashion shows; twisting; aerobics, discos; cigarette smoking; Olympics; riots; food rationing; coffee houses; rock concerts; world fairs; Times Square.
650 8		‡a World history ‡v Software.
651 8		‡a United States ‡x History ‡y 1900-1999 (20th century) ‡v Software.
700 1		‡a Ali, Waleed, ‡d 1950-
700 1		‡a Ali, Malik B.
700 1		‡a Zucaro, Lou.
700 1		‡a McGinty, Sean.
710 2		‡a MPI Multimedia.
710 1		‡a United States. ‡b Works Projects Administration.

CHAPTER 9
CATALOGING INTERACTIVE MULTIMEDIA

Cataloging rules for interactive multimedia are still evolving. This format does not appear in AACR2R. The first guidelines for cataloging interactive multimedia were published by the American Library Association in 1994:

> *Guidelines for Bibliographic Description of Interactive Multimedia*, by the Interactive Multimedia Guidelines Review Task Force, Laurel Jizba, et al. Chicago: American Library Association, 1994.

The guidelines combine some aspects of kits (300 field, Chief Source of Information, date) with some aspects of computer software (538 System Requirements, Source of Title Note). However, cataloging rules for interactive multimedia may soon change (see below). Until then, the above guidelines should be used.

What is Interactive Multimedia?

Interactive multimedia uses computer technology (microcomputer and/or Level III or higher videodisc player). Older interactive multimedia may consist of a videodisc with accompanying computer disks that help the user access the videodisc in various ways. Newer interactive multimedia may be a CD-ROM computer file which allows users to access the information at random and manipulate it in various ways, such as through hyperlinks.

Every item that says "interactive" may not qualify as interactive multimedia. The following types of items would not qualify: Level I and II videodiscs with barcode scanning list and no accompanying computer software; computer-assisted instruction or design; electronic books with text, audio, and/or graphics presented in linear fashion; video games with predetermined software paths; CD-ROMs with multiple media if navigation is only by menu options. To truly qualify as interactive multimedia, the item must use computer technology, must be user-controlled, and must contain nonlinear navigation. It must also contain a combination of two or more media (such as video segments, text, graphics, sound). If in doubt, do _not_ consider the item or package as interactive multimedia, and catalog the predominant medium with accompanying material (e.g., as a videodisc with accompanying barcode list, or as a computer file with accompanying user's guide, etc.). More detailed guidelines are found in *Guidelines for Bibliographic Description of Interactive Multimedia*.

Chief Source of Information

The Chief Source of Information is the entire work, all components and accompanying printed material, as it is for kits. Use the title that applies to the whole work or that appears to be a collective title. Prefer the source with the most complete title information, possibly the user's guide or container. Always include a 500 Source of Title Note, as for computer files.

GMD (245 ‡h)

The official GMD for interactive multimedia is currently **[interactive multimedia]**, _if_ the item truly meets the defined requirements. This new GMD has been used for only a few years. It received an unofficial sanction as an experimental GMD for use in OCLC records by U.S. libraries, but it was never officially approved. Many AV catalogers have been using this GMD, but it does not appear in the 1998 revision of AACR2R. The newest version of *ISBD(ER): International Standard Bibliographic Description for Electronic Resources*, now nearing the end of the approval process, is expected to replace the GMDs **[computer file]** and **[interactive multimedia]** with the more generic **[electronic resource]**. Watch for word of an official change. Until then, use **[computer file]** or **[interactive multimedia]** as appropriate. The entire ISBD(ER) may be accessed at: http://www.ifla.org/VII/s13/pubs/isbd.htm.

Statement of Responsibility (245 ‡c)

The Statement of Responsibility should include only persons or corporate bodies with <u>overall</u> responsibility for the entire interactive multimedia work. There is not always a Statement of Responsibility (245 ‡c) for interactive multimedia. Often the individual components have separate statements of responsibility. These belong in notes (persons in 508 field, corporate bodies in 500 note before the 508).

Edition Statement (250 field)

Look for an edition statement that relates to the work as a <u>whole</u> and record any other edition statements (as for one component) in a note. <u>Always</u> give the source of the edition statement (250 field) in a 500 note. The note about source of edition may be combined with the note about source of title, such as:

    500   **‡a Title and ed. from disc label.**

Computer File Characteristics (256 field)

As stated in the previous chapter, the 256 field, Computer File Characteristics, is defined as mandatory for computer software. But in practice, most catalogers do not use it except for Internet resources (if the information is known). The Library of Congress does not use the 256 field either. However, in the newest version of the *ISBD(ER): International Standard Bibliographic Description for Electronic Resources* are several new examples for this area. For interactive multimedia, the 256 field may state **Electronic interactive multimedia**. If the new ISBD(ER) is adopted, the 256 field may be important to distinguish interactive multimedia since the new GMD will be **[electronic resource]**.

Date (260 ‡c)

Various components of the interactive multimedia work may have different dates. Following the same rule as for kits, use the <u>latest</u> copyright date as the date in the imprint area of the cataloging record (260 ‡c). Some catalogers include 500 notes listing the varying dates and where they appear.

Physical Description (300 field)

If the interactive multimedia work is contained in a single physical carrier, such as a CD-ROM disc with a guide, record the physical description as appropriate for that physical carrier. If there is more than one physical carrier, list the physical components in the Physical Description Area (300 field) in the same way as components in a kit, separated by commas, including necessary physical details (such as floppy disk size) in parentheses. Watch the spelling of disc/disk: use **disc** for computer optical technology (usually CD-ROMs), and **disk** for computer magnetic technology (usually floppies). Use 5XX notes for more extensive physical details of components as needed.

Notes (5XX fields)

The first note should be a 538 System Requirements Note as for computer software, listing needed equipment for use of the item. The next note should be a 500 Source of Title Note (mandatory). If there is an edition statement (250 field), combine a note telling the <u>source</u> of the edition statement with the 500 Source of Title Note. Notes about varying titles (500 field) will follow. Next will be 500 notes about responsible corporate bodies, then notes about persons not listed in 245 ‡c. A 511 Cast or Performer Note or a 508 Credits Note can be used if needed (e.g. when there are video segments). Next, include 500 notes about important physical details that could affect use of the work, e.g.: **Can be used on Level I without the computer or on Level III with the computer.** Include a 520 Summary Note describing the item. A 505 Contents Note can be used to list the individually titled parts of the interactive multimedia work.

Subject Headings and Added Entries

Choose subject headings based on the content of the work. Sears has a new 650 subject heading for interactive multimedia, **Multimedia systems**, and the Library of Congress has a 650 subject heading, **Interactive multimedia**. However, these subject headings are intended for works <u>about</u> interactive multimedia, not for the form itself. Some catalogers borrow the Library of Congress form subdivision ‡v **Interactive multimedia** to subdivide topical Sears subject headings for this specialized format. It might also be useful for patrons if each subject heading were also entered with the subdivision **Software**. Interactive multimedia as a format seems to be merging into other electronic resources through upcoming changes in the new ISBD(ER). It is certain that the software aspect of interactive multimedia will remain important, while the interactive aspect may not always be considered a separate feature.

Added entries should be as for other nonbook materials. Trace responsible persons and corporate bodies, including publishers.

Note: Most of the above information was based on *Guidelines for Bibliographic Description of Interactive Multimedia*, the proposed ISBD(ER), and information from a conference and newsletter of the Online Audiovisual Catalogers (OLAC).

Examples follow.

Example of interactive multimedia on CD-ROM. The 300 field describes the predominant medium (main physical carrier) with accompanying printed item.

245 00		‡a Composer quest ‡h [interactive multimedia] : ‡b an interactive multimedia CD ROM.
246 30		‡a Quest
260		‡a Needham, MA : ‡b Dr. T's Music Software, ‡c c1991.
300		‡a 1 computer optical disc : ‡b sd., col. ; ‡c 4 3/4 in. + ‡e 1 leaflet.
538		‡a System requirements: Multimedia PC or equivalent; MS-DOS or PC-DOS 3.1 or later; Microsoft Windows with Multimedia Extensions 1.0; Microsoft MS-DOS CD-ROM extensions (MSCDEX) version 2.2 or later; 30MB hard disk; CD-ROM drive; audio board; mouse.
500		‡a Title from disc label.
508		‡a Conceived and developed by Jeff Pucci and Richard Viard ; programmed by Richard Viard.
520		‡a Interactive multimedia program on CD-ROM. Enables the user to investigate the greatest composers in classical and early jazz music, from the year 1600 into the 20th century. Features "learn" mode for free investigation of musical periods and styles, and "play" mode for a fun and challenging adventure game. Includes musical performances, biographies, news events from 1600 to present, major visual art styles and artists, musical trivia, quizzes, on-line help, definitions of musical terms, quick index to composers, and paintings and important developments in the world of art.
650 8		‡a Composers ‡v Interactive multimedia.
650 8		‡a Music ‡x History and criticism ‡v Interactive multimedia.
650 8		‡a Jazz music ‡x History and criticism ‡v Interactive multimedia.
650 8		‡a Art ‡x History ‡v Interactive multimedia.
650 8		‡a Educational games.
700 1		‡a Pucci, Jeff.
700 1		‡a Viard, Richard.
710 2		‡a Dr. T's Music Software.

Catalog card version:

Composer quest [interactive multimedia] : an interactive multimedia
CD-ROM. -- Needham, MA : Dr. T's Music Software, c1991.
1 computer optical disc : sd., col. ; 4 ¾ in. + 1 leaflet.

System requirements: Multimedia PC or equivalent; MS-DOS or
PC-DOS 3.1 or later; Microsoft Windows with Multimedia Extensions
1.0; Microsoft MS-DOS CD-ROM extensions (MSCDEX) version 2.2
or later; 30 MB hard disk; CD-ROM drive; audio board; mouse.
Title from disc label.
Credits: Conceived and developed by Jeff Pucci and Richard Viard
; programmed by Richard Viard.

 (Continued on next card)

Composer quest [interactive multimedia] ... c1991.   (Card 2)

Summary: Interactive multimedia program on CD-ROM. Enables
the user to investigate the greatest composers in classical and early jazz
music, from the year 1600 into the 20th century. Features "learn" mode
for free investigation of musical periods and styles, and "play" mode
for a fun and challenging adventure game. Includes musical
performances, biographies, news events from 1600 to present, major
visual art styles and artists, musical trivia, quizzes, on-line help,
definitions of musical terms, quick index to composers, and paintings
and important developments in the world of art.

 (Continued on next card)

Composer quest [interactive multimedia] ... c1991.   (Card 3)

1. Composers--Interactive multimedia. 2. Music--History and
criticism--Interactive multimedia. 3. Jazz music--History and
criticism--Interactive multimedia. 4. Art--History--Interactive
multimedia. 5. Educational games. I. Pucci, Jeff. II. Viard, Richard.
III. Dr. T's Music Software. IV. Title: Quest.

Example of interactive multimedia on CD-ROM, containing resources that users can manipulate to create presentations.

037   ‡a FFH 6615 ‡b Films for the Humanities & Sciences

245 00   ‡a Victorian Britain ‡h [interactive multimedia].

260   ‡a [Princeton, N.J.] : ‡b Films for the Humanities & Sciences, ‡c [1997], c1996.

300   ‡a 1 computer optical disc : ‡b sd., col. ; ‡c 4 ¾ in. + ‡e 1 installation guide (2 p. ; 13 cm.).

538   ‡a System requirements: Multimedia PC; at least 4 MB RAM (8 MB or more recommended); 2 MB free hard disk space; Windows 3.x or 95; monitor with at least a 256-color display; double speed or higher CD-ROM drive; sound card.

500   ‡a Title from disc label.

500   ‡a From preliminary screens: AVP Picturebase. -- Version 1.08.10. -- Chepstow, Monmouthshire, UK : AVP, c1996.

500   ‡a CD-ROM disc contains databases of text, images and sound that are controlled by the AVP PictureBase software (included on disc).

520   ‡a Resource materials that enable the user to be introduced to life in Victorian Britain and its legacy to the present day. Pictures in the database are accompanied by descriptive text and sound, and the themes can be traced by means of keyword searching. Users can manipulate the text and images to create presentations.

651 8   ‡a Great Britain ‡x Civilization ‡v Interactive multimedia.

651 8   ‡a Great Britain ‡x History ‡y 1800-1899 (19th century) ‡v Interactive multimedia.

710 2   ‡a Films for the Humanities (Firm)

710 2   ‡a AVP (Firm)

740 02   ‡a AVP Picturebase.

740 02   ‡a Picturebase.

Example of interactive multimedia on CD-ROM. The subject heading Dissection **is borrowed from the Library of Congress since there is no comparable Sears heading. Names of animals can be added as Sears headings if they are not listed in Sears.**

245 00   ‡a Learning all about dissection ‡h [interactive multimedia].

250   ‡a MS-DOS version.

260   ‡a Fairfield, CT : ‡b Queue, Inc. ; ‡a [Chicago, Ill.] : ‡b Clearvue, Inc., ‡c c1993.

300   ‡a 1 computer optical disc : ‡b sd., col. ; ‡c 4 ¾ in. + ‡e 1 user's guide (1 folded sheet).

538   ‡a System requirements: MS-DOS computer or compatible; 640K minimum RAM; 750K of hard drive space; additional 900K of hard drive space if program is installed on hard disk; VGA or MCGA monitor; external or internal CD-ROM drive; Soundblaster card or compatible.

500   ‡a Title from disc label; ed. from user's guide.

521 8   ‡a For junior and senior high school students.

520   ‡a Interactive CD-ROM program. Introduces animal dissection procedures and gives an overview of dissection as a scientific tool. Interactive media tutorial presents color photographs of actual dissections and includes in-depth studies of the earthworm, crayfish, fish, frog, and fetal pig. Includes a question mode that requires student responses before continuing, and records student scores in a class record file.

650 0   ‡a Dissection ‡v Interactive multimedia.

650 8   ‡a Earthworms ‡v Interactive multimedia.

650 8   ‡a Crayfish ‡v Interactive multimedia.

650 8   ‡a Fishes ‡v Interactive multimedia.

650 8   ‡a Frogs ‡v Interactive multimedia.

650 8   ‡a Pigs ‡v Interactive multimedia.

710 2   ‡a Queue, Inc.

710 2   ‡a Clearvue, Inc.

Example of an early form of interactive multimedia: videodisc with separate computer disks. Components are listed in the 300 field as for a kit.

245 04 ‡a The cell biology videodisc ‡h [interactive multimedia] : ‡b motion and function of the living cell.

246 30 ‡a Motion and function of the living cell

250 ‡a NTSC version.

260 ‡a Seattle, Wash. : ‡b Videodiscovery, Inc., ‡c c1991.

300 ‡a 1 videodisc, 2 computer disks (5 1/4 in.), 1 image directory (92 p.), 1 quick reference index.

538 ‡a System requirements: Apple II computer; Pioneer videodisc player for CAV format; remote control or barcode reader.

546 ‡a English and Spanish narration on separate channels.

500 ‡a Title and ed. from image directory and videodisc container.

500 ‡a Produced in cooperation with IWF, Germany.

511 0 ‡a Spanish narration, Angela Torres-Henrick, Fausto Torres ; English narration, Grayson Capp, Terry Palasz.

508 ‡a Producer, Shaun Taylor.

500 ‡a IWF version released in 1984. NTSC version adds database of still images, a Spanish and American sound track, and a disc directory which cross references major American textbooks to the videodisc chapters.

500 ‡a Titles on Apple computer disks: Cell constituents/division ; Cell motility.

520 ‡a Interactive video program which explores the inner workings of the living cell. Includes 86 film segments and hundreds of still frames covering the major teaching areas: cell types, cell constituents, mitosis and cytokinesis, fission and cell motility. With live action footage on animal cells, plant cells, budding, multiple fission, protoplasmic streaming, migration of organelles, migration of pigment granules, flagellar motility and adaptation to passive displacement.

650 8 ‡a Cells ‡v Interactive multimedia.

650 8 ‡a Biology ‡v Interactive multimedia.

700 1 ‡a Taylor, Shaun.

710 2 ‡a Institut für den Wissenschaftlichen Film (Gottingen, Germany)

710 2 ‡a Videodiscovery, Inc.

740 02 ‡a Cell constituents/division.

740 02 ‡a Cell motility.

BIBLIOGRAPHICAL REFERENCES

Anglo-American Cataloguing Rules. 2nd ed., 1998 revision. Chicago: American Library Association, c1998.

Bibliographic Formats and Standards. 2nd ed. Online version. URL http://www.oclc.org/oclc/bib/toc.htm

Cataloging Internet Resources: A Manual and Practical Guide. Ed. Nancy B. Olson. 2nd ed. Dublin, Ohio: OCLC, c1997. URL http://www.oclc.org/oclc/man/9256cat/toc.htm

Interactive Multimedia Guidelines Review Task Force. *Guidelines for Bibliographic Description of Interactive Multimedia.* Chicago: American Library Association, 1994.

ISBD(ER): International Standard Bibliographic Description for Electronic Resources. Frankfurt am Main: IFLA Universal Bibliographic Control and International MARC Programme, Deutsche Bibliothek, 1997. Web version. URL http://www.ifla.org/VII/s13/pubs/isbd.htm

Olson, Nancy B. *Cataloging of Audiovisual Materials and Other Special Materials: a Manual Based on AACR2.* Ed. Sheila Intner, Edward Swanson. 4th ed. DeKalb, Ill.: Minnesota Scholarly Press, 1998.

Sears List of Subject Headings. Ed. Joseph Miller. 16th ed. New York: H.W. Wilson Company, 1997.

NOTES

NOTES

APPENDIX A
PREVIEW FORM FOR AV ITEMS

TITLE OF ITEM_____

Format   ___1/2" videocassette(s) (VHS)
(check one)   ___3/4" videocassette(s) (U-matic)
                        ___videodisc
                        ___filmstrip(s) with cassette(s)
                        ___filmstrip(s) with record(s)
                        ___slide set with cassette(s)
                        ___sound cassette tape(s)
                        ___record(s)
                        ___sound compact disc(s)
                        other_____

FOR VIDEOCASSETTES:
    Digital time where title frame appears_____
    If there is no title frame, check_____
    Digital time where credits begin at end of program_____

PHYSICAL DESCRIPTION FOR VIEWED PROGRAMS (Check as appropriate):
___col. only   Video formats only:
___b&w only   ___liveaction
___col. with some b&w sequences   ___animated
___b&w with some col. sequences   ___comb. liveaction/animated
                                      ___stills with narration
                                      ___closed captioned
                                      ___open captioned
                                      ___dialogue in non-English
                                          _____(language)
                                      ___English subtitles
                                      ___audio-described

DOES THE SUMMARY ON OR WITH THE ITEM PROVIDE AN ACCURATE DESCRIPTION OF
THE PROGRAM CONTENTS?

___YES   ___NO   ___NO SUMMARY PROVIDED

RUNNING TIME IN MINUTES AND SECONDS: (If there are two or more programs on a
videocassette, list the running time of EACH and the digital time where each begins and ends.)

IF THERE ARE ANY TECHNICAL PROBLEMS WITH THE PROGRAM, DESCRIBE THESE ON
THE BACK OF THIS SHEET (such as jerky or fuzzy pictures, trouble with sound track, faulty
closed captions, faulty synchronization of slide/filmstrip program with automatic sound track, etc.; for
videos, give digital time where problems occur). IF PROBLEMS ARE MAJOR, DO NOT CONTINUE
TIMING.

ON THE BACK OF THIS SHEET, NOTE HIGHLIGHTS OF THE PROGRAM AND ANY OTHER
INFORMATION WHICH SHOULD BE INCLUDED IN THE SUMMARY ON THE CATALOGING
RECORD.

APPENDIX B
VARIABLE MARC FIELDS OFTEN USED
FOR NONBOOK CATALOGING

Following are variable fields that you will often use for nonbook cataloging.

100   AUTHOR MAIN ENTRY

110   CORPORATE BODY MAIN ENTRY

240   UNIFORM TITLE WITH AUTHOR MAIN ENTRY (used mostly for music and literature)

245   TITLE AND TITLE-RELATED FIELDS (Title Proper, Other Title Info., GMD, Statement of Responsibility)

246   VARYING FORM OF TITLE

250   EDITION STATEMENT

260   PLACE, PUBLISHER, DATE

300   PHYSICAL DESCRIPTION

440   SERIES (traced)

490   SERIES (traced differently in 830)

500   GENERAL NOTE

505   CONTENTS NOTE

508   CREDITS NOTE

511   CAST NOTE OR PERFORMER NOTE

518   DATE/PLACE OF RECORDING

520   SUMMARY NOTE

521   TARGET AUDIENCE NOTE

538   SYSTEM REQUIREMENTS

546   LANGUAGE NOTE

600   PERSONAL NAME AS SUBJECT

610   CORPORATE BODY AS SUBJECT

650   SUBJECT HEADING (Topical)

651   PLACE AS SUBJECT

700   PERSONAL NAME ADDED ENTRY

710   CORPORATE BODY ADDED ENTRY

730   UNIFORM TITLE ADDED ENTRY (e.g., TV program)

740   TITLE ADDED ENTRY (ANALYTIC OR RELATED)

830   SERIES TRACED DIFFERENTLY FROM 490

ABOUT THE AUTHOR

Marilyn McCroskey is an Associate Professor of Library Science at Southwest Missouri State University in Springfield. She has been the AV Cataloger at Duane G. Meyer Library, Southwest Missouri State University, since 1981, and head of the Meyer Library Catalog Department since 1993. She also teaches graduate-level cataloging classes. She is a member of the NACO-AV Funnel Project, a national cooperative cataloging project in which participating catalogers are authorized to create original authority records for OCLC. She a member of the Library Science Curriculum Committee for the SMSU Department of Library Science, the College of Education Professional Educational Committee, and the College of Education Diversity Committee. She holds Masters' degrees in Library Science and English as well as a B.S. in Education degree. She was a school librarian (grades 7-12) for five years before joining the SMSU faculty in 1981.

She has presented workshops on AV cataloging at various local, state, and national conferences, and has served as a reviewer of AV materials for library publications. *Cataloging Nonbook Materials with AACR2R and MARC* was originally based on a 1992 AASL National Conference session handout.

In other activities related to education, she has been an elected member of the Marionville (Mo.) R-9 Board of Education since 1992, serving as Board Secretary for six years until her election as Board President in April 1999. She serves on the district's Technology Committee and Library Committee. After years of planning and one failed attempt, this small school district (700 students) passed a bond issue by only six votes in April 1999 to build a grade 7-12 library media center and computer lab (previously the district had only one library and computer lab for all grade levels), along with other improvements, including district-wide computer networking. This is the school from which she graduated, and she is very pleased to see these needed improvements become a reality.

She lives on an 80-acre dairy farm with her husband and two teenaged daughters. She also has a son who is an intensive care nurse, and three grandchildren.